Praise for

LOVE IN VAIN

"Reads like a great American novel . . . The definitive book of any kind on the gifted, eccentric blues legend."

—*Pitchfork*

"It's about time."

—**Bob Dylan**

"Finally someone has captured the central feel of this master musician and his times, and that man is Alan Greenberg. Take my word for it."

—**Keith Richards**

"Magnificently rendered . . . This is no mere biopic. [Greenberg's] Johnson is a changeling, flesh-and-blood but mutable and secretive, and he dwells in a world of workaday magic, where his meeting with the devil takes place at the moviehouse in front of a western, and where Charlie Patton's funeral turns into a ferocious soul-claiming contest between Johnson and the Rev. Sin-Killer Griffin. Greenberg not only evokes Johnson in a way that actually enlarges our view of him, he also depicts the blues world of the time, from Mississippi to Texas, in all its variegated splendor and misery."

—**Luc Sante,** *New York Review of Books*

"It may be the best movie you'll see all year—even if it's just inside your head."

—*Entertainment Weekly*

"*Love in Vain* has accomplished what I have tried to do for a long time: that is, to develop screenplays as a new genre of literature that has its own natural right of existence."

—**Werner Herzog**

"The resonances of Robert Johnson's mysterious life and equally mysterious death continue to echo through American music, from blues to country to rock to soul. Alan Greenberg has thoroughly researched and understood the facts of Robert Johnson's career, but more importantly he has boldly and brilliantly reimagined the myth. *Love in Vain* is surreal in the original sense of the word; it transforms the reality of Robert Johnson, his time, his place, and his art, into a super-reality—sharp and vivid yet as luminous and elusive as a dream."

—**Robert Palmer,** *New York Times*

"*Love in Vain* is a blazingly readable screenplay that I recommend without reservation."

—**Greil Marcus**

"A great, great screenplay."

—**David Lynch**

"*Love in Vain* is a masterpiece of historical significance."

—*Memphis Commercial-Appeal*

"Since facts about Robert Johnson are almost as hard to come by as facts about Shakespeare, Greenberg proposes to give flesh to myth instead . . . he makes it happen, too. Drenched in alcohol and bodily fluids, this is gut-bucket romanticism at its most credible. By imagining the Mississippi Delta's churches, shacks, cotton fields, and (especially) jooks so vividly, Greenberg helps us see and hear why blues buffs are obsessed with all that raunch and suffering transport."

—Robert Christgau

"A quantum leap of the imagination."

—Dave Marsh

"Wondrous and vivid."

—*Portland Tribune*

"The really remarkable thing about *Love in Vain* is the way it plays off the mystery of Robert Johnson rather than attempt to penetrate it in literal terms. The screenplay represents the imaginative embodiment of a world, a world of myth and reality, both prosaic and poetic, a world in which Robert Johnson, or perhaps the *idea* of Robert Johnson, could spring up. I don't think this milieu has ever been effectively portrayed before, and I consider it little short of a miracle that Alan Greenberg should have captured it so graphically, so colorfully, so dramatically."

—Peter Guralnick

LOVE IN VAIN

Love in Vain

A VISION OF ROBERT JOHNSON

Alan Greenberg

FOREWORD BY
Martin Scorsese

INTRODUCTION BY
Stanley Crouch

University of Minnesota Press
Minneapolis
London

Originally published in 1983 by Doubleday; second edition
published in 1994 by Da Capo Press.

First University of Minnesota Press edition, 2012

Copyright information for song lyrics by Robert Johnson is
reproduced at the end of the book.

Published by the University of Minnesota Press
111 Third Avenue South, Suite 290
Minneapolis, MN 55401-2520
http://www.upress.umn.edu

Library of Congress Cataloging-in-Publication Data
Greenberg, Alan.
Love in vain : a vision of Robert Johnson / Alan Greenberg ;
foreword by Martin Scorsese ; introduction by Stanley Crouch.—
1st University of Minnesota Press ed.
Includes bibliographical references.
ISBN 978-0-8166-8080-1 (pb : alk. paper)
1. Johnson, Robert, d. 1938—Drama. 2. African American
musicians—Drama. 3. Blues musicians—Drama. I. Scorsese,
Martin. II. Crouch, Stanley. III. Title.
PN1997.3.G74 2012
791.43'6578—dc23
2012027595

Printed in the United States of America on acid-free paper

The University of Minnesota is an equal-opportunity educator
and employer.

19 18 17 16   10 9 8 7 6 5 4 3 2

DEDICATED TO THE MEMORY OF MY FATHER,
HOWARD ROOSEVELT GREENBERG

When I leave this town
I'm gonna bid you fair farewell
And when I return again you'll have
A great long story to tell.

CONTENTS

ACKNOWLEDGMENTS

The prior published draft of *Love in Vain* was written in early 1979 and was originally purchased by Mick Jagger as a work in progress. Since then, the story of the development of the screenplay and the subsequent film would make an engrossing book in itself. The author would like to thank the following people, living and departed, for their soulful support during this wild journey: Jeffrey Abelson, Nick Amster, Erik Anderson, Harry Belafonte, Stan Bickman, John Bloomgarden, Karen Boulegon, Marie Brown, Sarah Jane Buck-Amster, William S. Burroughs, Dr. Andy Chen, Sean Combs, Richard Cybulski, Stephen Davis, Michael Dean, Stuart Deutsch, James Luther Dickinson, Bob Dylan, Ward Emling, William Ferris, Melanie Friesen, Bill Gerber, Mike Golden, Bill Graham, Sid Graves, Howard and Beatrice Greenberg, Ona and Ry Greenberg, Paul Greenberg, Michael Gruener, Peter Guralnick, Werner Herzog, Larry Jackson, Jim Jarmusch, Alan Hans, Judith Hans-Price, Bob Katz, Dr. Ralph Kazer, Steve LaVere, Robert Lockwood Jr., David Lynch, Greil Marcus, Dan Margulis, Mack McCormick, Tim Blake Nelson, Robert Palmer, Prince, John Ré, Keith Richards, Richard Ringler, Bob Rose, Jane Rose, Jeff Rosen, Dr. Richard B. Rosen, Joe Ruffalo, Deborah Salkov, Jeff Scher, Andy Scott, Johnny Shines, John Stansifer, Yuval Taylor, Ron Thornhill, Daryl Vinson, Mary Vivian, Sterling Waiters, Jeff Werner, Jerry Winters, Michael Wright, and Dr. Alan Yesner.

FOREWORD TO THE
SECOND EDITION

Martin Scorsese

I REMEMBER first hearing about Robert Johnson at a time when all my friends who were serious about music seemed to be listening to the blues—the *real* stuff, guys like Blind Lemon Jefferson, Lightnin' Hopkins, Howlin' Wolf, Elmore James, B. B. King, and Muddy Waters. Of them all, Johnson was the most intriguing, perhaps because he was also the most obscure. The thing about Robert Johnson was that he only existed on his records. He was pure legend. Even the experts didn't have much of a clue as to who he really was—just that he recorded a total of twenty-nine songs, that he died young, and that he was the greatest Delta bluesman of all time. I think it was the combination of all these blues masterpieces and the complete absence of hard facts—the absolute mystery and the indisputable genius—that for me charged the Johnson legend with an irresistible appeal and attracted me to Alan Greenberg's remarkable screenplay.

With this issue of a second edition, it seems to me even more appropriate that *Love in Vain*, though as yet unproduced as a film, should be published in book form. For me the script reads like literature. Alan's unique style captures the Mississippi Delta in images of stark sensuality and a matter-of-fact pain and poverty that are the very essence of Johnson's music. In its mix of Depression-era realism with Southern black folklore, I see the script less as a literal history than as a spiritual biography. Johnson is like some haunted prophet who must go into the desert to find his voice, and who plays his music not out of choice but because he has no choice: he has become possessed by the spirit of the blues. That the script represents this possession as a literal pact with the devil (this was the legend of Johnson's extraordinary guitar skill) only speaks to the existential predicament of all artists and to one of the cruel paradoxes of human nature: that our finest art is born from the wellspring of pain.

New York City, 1993

PRINTING THE LEGEND

Stanley Crouch

> This is the West, sir. When the legend becomes fact,
> print the legend.
>
> —John Ford, *The Man Who Shot Liberty Valance*

I FIND IT FITTING that the first book written about Mississippi's Delta blues legend Robert Johnson is grounded as much in myth, legend, and tall tale as in research. The work's obvious inclination toward the fantastic and the cultural metaphors of superstition separates it from those largely fictional film biographies that are pushed forward as factual; it also proposes that we can learn as much from good mythology as from fine documentation—if the mythology carries or transmits how a world may have *felt* to those participants, onlookers, and descendants swept up in the lore of time and impatient with flat facts. The vision of *Love in Vain*, then, swells personality, circumstance, and action to the proportions of legend and propels that legend with such audacity and awe, humor and terror, sensuality and dread-laden sorrow that it is obvious how much the writer has been touched and inspired by the broad and mysterious passions of Robert Johnson's life and music.

Alan Greenberg's Robert Johnson is as much an American bard as the anonymous cowboys of the last century who created both Pecos Bill and the songs that filled the long nights under the big skies. This Robert Johnson appears as a figure we recognize yet find vastly mysterious. The consternation and outrage he inspires in the boyfriends of the local girls he charms through his exotic powers as drifting musician fall roughly into a familiar cinematic key. But he is mysterious because his gifts float his life and his art across the threshold of genius, where the beautiful can be as interwoven with the violent, the bloody, the courageous, and the painful as is childbirth. That his music can inspire or instigate contradictory passions and actions as far removed as love and murder—or appear to—adds to the mysterious, even dangerous qualities of the stranger this Robert Johnson remains throughout the work.

Yet Johnson's world also remains strange to the character himself, and it is a place in which he is no more comfortable by the end of his life than he was when we first met him. It is a universe made so cockeyed by constant drinking that reality is a series of dulled, sullenly received, or exuberantly pursued experiences. Much like a jungle, that jook-joint area of life contains the lovely and the predatory, most of them inebriated and stumbling into each other as love and violence bump and grind in a sweaty and impoverished half-light. Robert Johnson's delicate relationship to it all makes him a tragic character, for the essence of the tragic flaw is that it dooms by throwing the hero out of step with the world. The human significance of the tragic hero is measured by the nature of the character's emotional response to the situation. Robert Johnson's response was to narrate through the vehicle of music the dimensions of a sensibility both wooed and repulsed, appreciated and brutalized by a nightmare world.

The nature of Robert Johnson's nightmare, however, is much larger and more primal than the tools of sociology would allow us to explicate, for then we would only be led down the purple path of accusations based on economic and environmental shortcomings. All of those accusations are true, but they are not true enough to say more to us about the human condition than

Johnson's art of the blues, which is a music that shakes its fist at fate as often as it accepts the saddening upshots of bad decisions and bad luck. For the blues sensibility, the constant riddle is that of human joy and human dissatisfaction, and what the two have to do with human conduct. Yet because the erotic is seen through the blues in a broad and unsentimental fashion, its morality is far more stilted and very complex, with neither man nor woman the more driven or given to shady actions because of sexual desires. Consequently, the blues gives an epic sense of the erotic to American music and tears the cotton candy shroud from the boudoir, speaking of the elegant and the raw, the ennobling and the debilitating—all pushed down the listener's consciousness with often bittersweet and sardonic images. Only through an awareness of these things can we approach the nightmare of Robert Johnson with firmer footing than the sociological statistic.

The mythological is as firm a footing as any. The dilemma Alan Greenberg faced in creating his Robert Johnson was awesome because it called for depicting a man of genius who was also an intuitive artist and a product of a rough-and-tumble world not far removed from the disorder of cattle towns on cowboy weekends, logging camps, or the communities that grew up in the shadows of gold strikes. Johnson's aesthetic cartography made use of spirits and demons, images from the industrial world and from the marketplace, vulgar threats and dares from the hangouts of corner boys and thugs, all interlaced with phrases and themes passed on to him from his predecessors. The result was a vision as domestically surreal as tall tales or the "dozens." In fact, one could easily say that Robert Johnson shaped an art in which the tallest tales of human experience, whether wonderful or woeful, were equaled by a craftsmanship and imagination that elevated his work from the amorphous world of Delta Ned Buntlines to that of fish stories lining up to march on the universe of *Moby Dick*. His genius was that of the innovator: Johnson expanded the possibilities of his idiom through the creation and delivery of his lyrics and the rudely or tenderly beautiful gradations of his guitar playing. Like another domestic pioneer, Daniel Boone, his victories against the wilderness led to legends.

The segregated Southern society in which Robert Johnson developed contained, for all its Jim Crow laws, a kind of black frontier world that came into existence after nightfall. There black men and women could act as wildly as they wished as long as they didn't harm the lives or ownings of whites. Where the blues was invented, refined, and danced to, people who usually did hard, mindless, or boring work in cotton fields, sawmills, or turpentine farms and so on put on the dog. Just as the verbal imagination and legendary feats espoused by frontiersmen and cowboys were responses to harsh, impersonal difficulties, the jook-joint culture was also one of homemade glamour and glory. There black people dressed up, they strutted, they drank, they swore, they told tall tales and boasted; they also gambled and flirted, since money and flesh could be fast, loose, and recklessly used. Where Davy Crockett exemplified the frontier vision when he boasted, "I can walk like an ox, run like a fox, swim like an eel, yell like an Indian, fight like a devil, spout like an earthquake, make love like a mad bull, and swallow a nigger whole without choking if you butter his head and pin his ears back," Rudy Ray Moore recites the black equivalent when he says, "I was born in a barrel of butcher knives, I been shot in my ass with two Colt .45s, I been bit by a shark and stung by an eel, I chew up railroad iron and spit out steel." Bluesman Peetie Wheatstraw called himself "the Devil's son-in-law" and "the high sheriff of Hell." In one song, Robert Johnson chants, "I'm going to upset your backbone, put your kidneys to sleep, do the breakaway on your liver, and dare your heart to beat!"

The development of the blues itself parallels the evolution of popular nineteenth-century characters and forms like minstrelsy; both were responses to the growing feeling of group identity among lower-class rural whites who had come to the cities and wanted art that addressed their experience through dramatic parable, monologue, melodrama, satire, or skit. In the backwoods of the Delta blues, the art could be crude, even rude, but it wasn't to be pretentious or given to sentimentality, probably a secular vision of the attitude that had led slaves to strip flowery language and notes from the Christian hymns when they learned them. It is possible that the rough texture of life could only be countered by religious or secular art forged with the spirit of steel, not the tin of the maudlin. The inner workings of human lives were at issue and, as Albert Murray says in *Stomping the Blues*, "The spirit, after all, is not only what is threatened but is also the very part of you that is assumed to be the most vulnerable. For what is ultimately at stake is morale, which is to say the will to persevere, the disposition to persist and perhaps prevail; and what must be avoided by all means is a failure of nerve." So blues became a narration and an interpretation of experience, a music of courtship and battle cries that was performed for demanding and often dangerous audiences, or audiences that frequently included violent and dangerous men and women.

Even though he was the king of this rough-and-tumble carnival, the bluesman was not above danger, and those dangers he faced had much to do with what he provided on one hand and represented on another. The bluesman supplied the musical background against which hearts were won or broken; he was the unknown drifter, or the notorious one. He could raise the dance and erotic fevers of his listeners and express, in however limited a way, another level of sophistication than that of the ordinary workingman at the jook joint trying to have a good time. A traveler, he sometimes came to town with new slang, predicted in his dress future fashion, and dazzled the girls, many of whom were primed for almost anything that suggested excitement beyond what little they'd come to expect from everyday life. At the height of the evening, a familiar man had the chance to be moved by and abandoned for the music-making stranger. If the girl was the wrong one, the bluesman could feel physical wrath from the girl herself, a boyfriend, a relative. The balance was always a proverbially delicate one.

Love in Vain shapes its tale around the problems of balance and, in the rendering of Robert Johnson's drives and adventures, gives us a vision as elemental and subtle as that of a fine Western. Its themes and struggles come together as a tall-tale nightmare tragedy filled with aesthetic gunfights, camaraderie, raw or melodramatic romance, comic characters, satire and figures that prove out the slave hymn adage, "Old Satan is a liar and a conjuror, too; if you don't mind, he'll conjure you." But in this case the ambitious young man doesn't desire the position of top gun, biggest rancher, best horseman or such; he wants to be the best Delta blues musician. The introduction of a Faustian element connects perfectly to the black folk belief that the blues was the Devil's music and its practitioners hellbound. It also suggests, in perfect mythic keeping, that supreme creation can be some sort of a challenge to the gods and can result from a pact with dark forces. Before Johnson reaches the tragic consequences of his deal, we are given many images of darkness, or night, as the liberating province of tender desires, genial celebration, and the savage moods of the destructive. The writer does a fine job of showing Johnson's personality slowly dissolve as the character of his music becomes more distinctive and innovative, as if the art came to replace a soul thrown bloody lump by bloody lump on to the fiery breast of the Devil.

LOVE IN VAIN

LOVE IN VAIN

1. EXT. COTTON FIELD AND CHURCH — NIGHT

A hard rain, and the tiny white clapboard church on the edge of the field glows softly by candlelight from within. There, an entranced choir of female voices coos and moans hypnotically.

A stout black woman steps out the side door into the downpour. She picks up an ax beneath the chinaberry tree and hustles about, chopping hard at the rain and the muddy ground. From inside the church, the voice of the PREACHER rises above his choir.

> PREACHER (O.S.)
>
> Brothers and sisters, in being a duty-bound servant of God I stand before you tonight to try to bring you a message of "Thus sayeth the Lord." Seems I'm hoarse some now with the cold, but if you'll stick by me a little while and God is willing we will preach. You know the hounds of hell are so fast on our trail we got to go sometime, whether we like it or not. So here we are tonight, to hear what the spirit has to say. . . .

The rain subsides; the stout woman stops her chopping and reenters the church.

3

SUPER: The Mississippi Delta, near Robinsonville, 1930

2. EXT. GRAVEL ROAD — NIGHT

One last rumble of thunder leaves a wet and ghostly stillness. From far down the road comes a glimmering of headlights; we hear the sputtering of a jalopy, and the mud. When the old car lumbers into view, it stalls. Two aged black sharecroppers get out and step to the front of the car.

Chewing on a wad of tobacco, the DRIVER checks beneath the hood. With his back to the driver, the PASSENGER urinates onto the roadside while telling a story.

> PASSENGER
> . . . when they was out in the field workin.' Overseer say they ain't much good, gonna tie 'em up an' whip 'em. But they say, "Mr. Overseer, you ain't gonna lick me," an' runs to the river. Overseer he sure thought he catch 'em when he get there, only 'fore he get to 'em they rise up in the air an' fly away. Fly right back to Africa. Yessuh. Yonder past Friars Point—

> DRIVER
> Le's push.

The driver spits a jawful of black tobacco juice as they head for the rear of the car, where a long bundle is strapped across the trunk: the dead body of a young black man.

A haunting music, Blind Willie Johnson's 1927 "Dark Was the Night, Cold Was the Ground," descends from the clouds. The two skinny men push the jalopy up the road as others filter onto the road from the fields. These sharecroppers glance at the car and body tied behind while proceeding in the opposite direction. Slowly we follow. The music ensues as the titles appear.

SUPER: LOVE IN VAIN

The anonymous figures step off the road toward the middle of a grim cotton field where a strange shack made of rusted sheet metal stands. The dilapidated place sparkles from the rich amber light of dampered kerosene lamps inside. Around the shack, bottle lamps with rope wicks flicker, throwing angry shadows off the trees with sagging limbs.

We creep closer as the music fades. The joint is jammed with sharecroppers. There is feverish dancing inside and out.

3. INT. JOOK JOINT — NIGHT

Images of chaos, of rough black bodies rubbing and sweating and dancing wildly in the heated kerosene haze, powered by a loud pounding rhythm raging with erotic dread. Walls painted randomly in harsh dark shades close in on the shocking scene. People are half seen, acts are half followed, as in dreams.

Seated on a chair amid the tumult, a stocky man named WILLIE BROWN frantically knots a broken string on his guitar. In the corner his partner SON HOUSE fends off a woman who keeps pouring beer into his battered guitar. Son guzzles the beer out of his guitar until it is dry, as Willie yells to him.

WILLIE
Son, take over! Hey Son, take over now quick!

The furious momentum increases even without the music. Son rushes toward Willie as his female admirer chugs the rest of her beer. Picking up on the sizzling tempo by stomping his foot and sliding a jagged glass bottleneck over the guitar strings, Son explodes with improvised song.

SON
No use hollerin', no use screamin' an' cryin' / Y'know you got a home, mama, long as I got mine!

Willie tightens the knotted string and trades verses with Son, shouting out the song with all his might.

> WILLIE
>
> *I start to kill my woman till she lay down 'cross the bed / She looked so ambitious I took back everything I said!*

The air is ecstatically wicked. The intense activity is a cross between heated dance and heavy petting. One woman struts like a chicken as her mate makes a face like a fish. Others pound the walls with fists and bones. One guy grabs onto a window and jerks it off its hinges. The surging music ensues.

4. EXT. JOOK JOINT — NIGHT

A local bootlegger's makeshift bar is crowded by jook patrons. ROBERT JOHNSON, a slender nineteen-year-old dressed in striped pants with suspenders, a clean white shirt and two-toned wingtip shoes, watches the bootlegger fill his soda bottle with hootch.

Robert walks to the edge of the yard. He empties his bottle in three or four turns, then stares out at the whispering field. After a few seconds he heads back to the hootch stand.

A lanky, mustachioed youth named GOAT marches into the yard towing his pretty but lame girlfriend LAVENDAR in a homemade wooden wagon. Lavendar beckons Goat as they pass the stand.

> LAVENDAR
>
> Say, Babyface . . . oh, Goat—

> GOAT
>
> Don't got the change.

LAVENDAR

What do you got.

GOAT

You, babe.

Goat parks the wagon near Robert's vacated spot. Lavendar remains standing in the wagon as he eyes the jook.

GOAT

Be right back.

LAVENDAR

You gonna jook some, Goat? That ain't fair since I got this leg.

GOAT

Quiet now, Lavendar. Just gonna fix us up some shoeshine. I be right back.

LAVENDAR

You gonna dance in there, I know it. Ain't you, Goat? Ain't you, Babyface? Say, Goat—

Goat approaches the shack, ignoring Lavendar. Robert passes Goat with his bottle of corn liquor.

GOAT (LOW)

All set? Harp wet?

Robert nods almost imperceptibly to Goat and resumes his drunken vigil as Lavendar shouts out a popular blues.

LAVENDAR

I say jake leg jake leg jake leg jake leg / Tell me what in the world you gonna do—

Lavendar performs atop her wagon, bellowing and writhing. Robert continues drinking, oblivious to her. His steady deep-set eyes, now glazed, reflect a precarious inner resolve.

LAVENDAR

Mama mama mama cried out an' said, / "Oh, Lord, ain't there somethin' in this world po' daddy can do"—

Ogling Robert, she stops singing. She rests her stiff leg over the wagon's edge and poses with hand on hip. A strap on her thread-bare red dress slips off her bony shoulder.

LAVENDAR

Where's that Goat? Where's my Hooky Doodle? Motherin' sonofabitch. In there jookin' with some free-fuckin' whores givin' out pussy they can't even sell. I'll kill 'im. That Goat he got a thang so long they gonna jack 'im off to let the coffin lid down.

Robert ignores her.

LAVENDAR

Say, Robert Johnson, now isn't that so? Say, Robert Johnson, how 'bout you?

He swigs some hootch and continues gazing upon the field.

LAVENDAR

Huh? Ain't that you, Robert Johnson? Good boy Robert Dusty? Good boy Robert Dusty never seen his papa's face? You come here Rusty Dusty an' tote Lavendar to Hooky Doodle's door over yonder.

Robert, perturbed, ignores Lavendar while finishing off his hootch. He holds the empty bottle and stares.

LAVENDAR

Hmmm. A bastard. You a bastard if there ever was one, Robert Johnson. You never seen his face 'cause I know you never seen 'im. Yo' papa's name was Noah. Yo' mama, huh, she mightn't've married no Noah, an' that's a fact, but sweet Julia an' ol' Noah musta done somethin' *bad* 'cause there you *is*. Say, Robert Johnson, there you is.

Robert walks over and faces Lavendar.

ROBERT

You tote yourself.

LAVENDAR (SOFTLY)

Set you on fire, Robert.

Robert tosses the bottle aside and walks toward the jook. She looks at him and spits.

LAVENDAR

Guess Lavendar best go find ol' Goat herself.

As Robert enters the jook's side door, Lavendar limps after him, towing her wooden wagon. At the side door she steps back onto the little wagon and stands alone, as before.

5. INT. JOOK KITCHEN — NIGHT

A tight alcove with Goat and three women, dipping snuff and drinking. Goat, a grotesque bloody hare's foot dangling from his neck, pours a can labeled "Shoe Shine" through a slice of white bread into a tin cup to filter the liquid polish clear.

An inebriated WOMAN with sinking eyelids clutches onto Goat as he tastes his brew; they grin beatifically. Robert pushes through as Goat balances two full cups, heading for the door.

> LAVENDAR (O.S.)
>
> *I say jake leg jake leg jake leg jake leg*—What the hell's goin' on!

> WOMAN
>
> Aw, Goat, you keep givin' her that shoeshine stuff'll kill her some day—an' I be here waitin'! Mmmmmm, come to mama—

6. INT. JOOK JOINT — NIGHT

Bedlam reigns in flickering lamplight as Willie and Son play on. Willie spots Robert by the door and frowns. Tapping his brow with a clean white kerchief that glows in the flickering amber, Robert's eyes are fixed upon the musicians.

> WILLIE
>
> *Jinx all 'round, jinx all 'round my bed / Got up this mornin' an' it likened to kill me dead—*

As Robert moves through the crowd a burly man lifts a sexy wench onto a table. Someone lights a candle and sets it between her bare feet as she bumps and grinds.

Robert sits on the floor at the musicians' feet. As Robert studies Willie's hands, ornery Willie glares back.

> WILLIE
>
> What's it say, Little Robert?

The wench squats and flirts with the flame as aroused male voices shout encouragement.

WILLIE

What's it say, Little Robert? You hear it? Where's yo' harp?

ROBERT

Don't blow no harp.

WILLIE

Where's yo' harp at?

ROBERT

Play gui-tar now.

WILLIE

Take a man to play gui-tar, boy—

SON

Blues ain't nothin' but a low-down shakin' chill. / If you ain't had 'em, honey, hope you never will—

His hands cupped over his mouth, Robert suddenly explodes with a brilliant, biting wail on his harmonica.

Son's left hand streaks across the guitar neck, bleeding badly, cut from the jagged glass bottleneck. He plays on.

In one abrupt swoop the wench dips down and picks up the burning candle between her legs. The jook erupts in cheers.

WILLIE

So what's it say, Robert—can't you tell? Ain't you sayin'?

When Son's female admirer pours hootch on his bleeding hand, with a loud yelp he leaps to his feet and pushes his way out.

Robert eyes Son's fallen guitar, his white shirt spotted with blood. As Willie glares at Robert, he plucks a string hard and snaps it. Instantly Robert pounces on Son's guitar and sits with it facing the wall.

> WILLIE
>
> Damn it, Robert, lay it down!

In the eye of the thunderous storm, Robert cradles the guitar as if it were alive, struggling with it, squeezing it to emit sound. When Willie lunges at him, Robert ducks away, and, now hooting and hollering madly, he starts swinging Son's guitar over his head in the smoke-filled, flickering maelstrom.

Son rushes back to see his guitar flying. Punches are thrown. Robert crawls across the floor and grabs the kerosene lamp.

7. EXT. JOOK JOINT — NIGHT

The light goes out in the jook. Perched atop her odd wagon under the lone burning lamp, Lavendar exults in the night.

> LAVENDAR
>
> Whoa, California! He's blowed it up with that stuff!
> He's blowed it up!

8. EXT. COTTON FIELD — MIDNIGHT

Leaving the noisy jook behind, Son and Willie trek home through the high stalks.

> WILLIE
>
> Sure am glad Charley showed.

SON

But you catch that decoration? Clown's got a lick so dizzy take a three-legged man to dance to it.

WILLIE

He's a great man, that Charley Patton, he's a great big man—

SON

Hushhh . . . .

Robert is kneeling on the ground amid the stalks, bent over, near tears. Son and Willie stand quietly over him.

WILLIE (LOW)

Black nigger baby gonna take care of hisself.

SON (LOW)

It's up to you.

Gently they lift Robert up by his arms. Robert slips his white kerchief into a pocket and brushes himself off.

ROBERT

Moon comin' round now—

From high overhead, an aerial view of the livid shifting clouds above the horizon and the slumbrous fields below. Three tiny figures walk toward shacks a few fields away.

SON

Robert, you all right. Ain't that so, Willie Brown. You jus' do yo' best 'cause there ain't no better place to do yo' best than right here in the U. S. of A. Work hard, even down here in Mississippi, you get whatever it is you want. Same over in Arkansas, Lou'siana an' Memphis.

WILLIE

Best stay 'way from Alabama, though. Lotsa dead folk. Act like heathens down there—folks stomp all over you.

SON

That's right—jus' do yo' best. Don't say nothin' 'bout no one. Stay the place you're in, where you're told. Get down on yourself, forget it 'cause remember now, this is a free enterprise *system* we got here—

FADE OUT.

9. EXT. MISSISSIPPI RIVER — MORNING

The great river is visible in a soft blue curving sweep, as the hypnotic sound of distant sharecroppers chanting in the fields drifts in. The song is sung not in chorus but as a swelling up of harmonizing solos. The melody ranges from a minor note of despair to a triumphant major.

FIELD SINGERS

Captain, I due to be in Monroe / Ohhhh, in them long, hot summer days—

10. EXT. COTTON FIELDS — MORNING

A vast blinding whiteness of cotton over a sea of green, with scattered figures of black workers moving against it in bold relief. The stark cadence of voices continues.

FIELD SINGERS (CONT.)

Black gal, if I never more see you / Ohhhh, in them long, hot summer days—

Men, women and children stoop in the awful heat, pulling seedy cotton from the bolls and stuffing it into long white sacks. Their movements are graceful and rhythmic; the workers are entranced so to cope.

We see Goat across the field on a cloud of picked cotton in a mule-drawn wagon. He hollers out a blues, playing his guitar. Seventy-five yards closer in, spindly HENRY SIMS, 45, picks apart a testy boll. He retreats so that cross-eyed, balding T-BONE JONES, 40, can chop it with his hoe.

Robert stares blankly at his hoe as it hacks a boll. The itinerant country preacher ELDER HADLEY shouts his prayer and sermon from the field's edge, sixty yards away.

ELDER HADLEY

O Almighty beloved Father, we pray here 'neath Your high fields of mercy, bowed down at Your footstool so to thank You for these earthly lives. An' for gettin' us Your childrens up this mornin' clothed in our right minds—

Sweating heavily, eyes staring down at his hoe, spellbound Robert chops and chops as the preacher proceeds.

A white pickup truck turns onto the gravel road rimming the field and slowly approaches the preacher.

ELDER HADLEY

O Lord our Captain King, please give to us a restin' place where we can praise Thy name forever, for

sweet Jesus our Redeemer's sake, forever thank God
and Amen.

The pickup stops. Two middle-aged white men, the pinkish,
red-haired plantation FOREMAN, pistol on hip, and dark-haired,
clerkish HENRY SPEIR, get out and head for the preacher.

ELDER HADLEY

My brothers an' sisters, my subject for this mornin' is,
"The World Is in a Hell of a Fix"—I mean *this* world's
in a hell of a fix! These are dyin' days! These are
perilous times! We livin' in times of the Businessman!
An' the Profiteer! An' the Bootlegger! An' the False
Pretender! Men have turned their backs on God!

FOREMAN

Say, Bishop—

ELDER HADLEY

God is calling! God is calling! The world is upside
down!

FOREMAN

Say, Preacher, say, Preach, whoa—let's cut that stuff
out so's we can be of some use, help me find that
no-good yodelin' overseer o' mine. You seen Goat?
Mr. Speir here from town's got some business to see
him on.

The preacher eyes Goat, still singing atop his wagon across the
field. He shifts his eyes and plays dumb.

ELDER HADLEY

Goat, you say?

FOREMAN

Goat. Bubber Rubberdick.

ELDER HADLEY

Sure is a strange name for a Christian. You got me,
Mr. Foreman. Lord knows where he is.

SPEIR

There, over yonder, I see 'im—Say, hey, Goat! Yahoo!
Say Bubber!

FOREMAN

Leave it to me, Speir—I'm the specialist in nigger
nature 'round here. (hollering) Hey, yahoo, Goat!
Say Bubber!

The foreman trots out toward the distant wagon.

11. EXT. COTTON WAGON — MORNING

Goat stands in the mass of cotton playing his guitar, his fly down,
singing and yodeling "Cool Drink of Water."

GOAT

*I asked for water, an' she give me gas-o-line / Cryin',
Lord, Lordy Lord—*

FOREMAN

Say, Goat!

In his panic Goat looks down at disheveled, sex-worn Lavendar,
writhing spread-eagled in the whiteness.

> GOAT

God dog, it's the foreman—

> LAVENDAR

Piss on 'im, Goat—go git 'im, you can do it, jus' don't think 'bout it none, go crack 'im now—

> FOREMAN

Down, Goat! Say down a minute now!

> LAVENDAR

Boy, you kick 'im 'til yo' shoes is shitty!

Goat drops the guitar over the side, hops down and lopes toward the foreman as Lavendar urges him on in song.

> LAVENDAR

You got to move, you got to move / You got to move, chile, you got to move—

Goat's guitar lies by a wheel. The mule eyes the guitar, then with its hoof crushes it, laughing and snorting wickedly.

12. EXT. COTTON FIELD — MORNING

The foreman and Goat walk peaceably across the field.

> FOREMAN

This fella Speir here from town's got some record business to see you on. Prob'ly wants you to go make 'im another hit somewheres.

> GOAT

'Scuse me, sir, but I can't make none o' them records no more—I sold away my rights. It was a real bad

deal, Mr. Foreman. I was drinkin' that denature an'
was on the kerosene when the Victor man come, an'
what he wanted was my rights. So I sold 'em. They
gone. Can't sing no more for no one.

> FOREMAN

You signed a recording contract with the Victor
company?

> GOAT

Got me six bucks. Cash. Had a pretty song to sing
'im, too. But yessir, I sold 'em my rights.

> FOREMAN (FADING DISTANTLY)

Them rights was for your *old* stuff, Goat. You go with
Speir so they can pay you for some *new* stuff.

13. EXT. COTTON FIELD — AFTERNOON

Never lifting his gaze, Robert still chops and chops hypnotically
in the brutal heat. At the field's edge the preacher rants on.

> ELDER HADLEY

God is CALLING! God is CALLING! It's HARD
TIMES we havin'! We got MILLIONS out o' work!
We got worldwide DEPRESSION! SO Y'BETTER
GET RIGHT WITH GOD!

Weary Lavendar, dozing in the cart behind Robert, wakens. She
buttons her blouse and glances around for Goat.

> ELDER HADLEY (CONT.)

YOU BETTER GET RIGHT 'CAUSE JESUS IS
RISING! JESUS IS RISING!

LAVENDAR (TO HERSELF)

Goat's gone.

Entranced Robert chops and chops as Lavendar rises beyond
him, her stiff leg propped atop the cotton mound.

ELDER HADLEY

GET RIGHT WITH GOD! GET RIGHT WITH
GOD!

LAVENDAR

CHRIST'S SAKE, ROBERT DUSTY, GOAT'S
GONE!

ELDER HADLEY

THESE ARE THEM LAST DAYS! THESE ARE
THEM LYIN' CRYIN' TIMES WHEN MEN
DESIRE MORE PLEASURE THAN THEY DO
MORE GOOD!

LAVENDAR

THEY GOT 'IM RUSTY DUSTY AN' HE'S GONE!
OH LORD I HATES TO PONDER SOME FAT-
BREASTED BITCH THAT'S SNORIN' IN MY
HOOKY DOODLE'S FACE!

As Robert chops on and on, gazing down, the rapid-fire voices
vying for his mind clash and converge in confusion overhead.

ELDER HADLEY

—SO YOU GOT TO ATONE! OH, THEM BULL
COWS COULDN'T DO IT! OH, THEM HEIFERS
AN' BLACK-BLOODED DOVES COULDN'T DO

IT! BUT GOD'S A-CALLIN'! Y'KNOW I HEAR
GOD A-CALLIN' ME RIGHT NOW!

LAVENDAR

—COME AN' GIT IT! YOU COMIN' RUSTY
DUSTY, FO' YO' PO' CHERRY RED? YOU COMIN'
OUT HERE TO THESE HIGH FIELDS? THESE
ARE THEM HIGH FIELDS, DUSTY! THESE ARE
THEM HIGH FIELDS!

ELDER HADLEY

—BUT NOW WAY UP IN HEAVEN FOR A
THOUSAND AND THOUSANDS OF YEARS,
THE SON WAS SAYIN' TO THE FATHER, "PUT
UP A SOUL! PREPARE ME A BODY! AN' I'LL GO
DOWN AN' MEET JUSTICE ON OL' CALVARY'S
BROW!"

Distantly an unruly mule is led off the field by a hand.

LAVENDAR

—SAY SOMETHIN', DUSTY! MY NERVES IS BAD!
MY NERVES IS BAD 'CAUSE I AIN'T DRINKIN'
ENOUGH, BUT DUSTY, YOU IS SIN-SICK! YOU'S
SIN-SICK AN' WON'T EVEN SIGNIFY!

Violently the mule breaks away, knocking the field hand down.

ELDER HADLEY

—OH-OO-OHHH! I SEED THE SUN WHEN SHE
TURN HERSELF BLACK AS THE NIGHT! I SEED
THE MOON WEEP AN' THE STARS A-FALLIN'
FROM THE SKY! OH, THE SAINTS ARE SINGIN'
AN' THE LORD'S CRYIN' OUT TO TESTIFY!

A puff of smoke in the far field and the pop of a gun. The irrepressible mule twists upward and drops.

LAVENDAR

ROBERT JOHNSON, YOU A COWARD!

14. EXT. COTTON FIELD — TWILIGHT

Abruptly, dazed, Robert chops hard with his hoe and sees a cottonmouth snake writhe in the dirt, cut in two. He looks up. The fields are hushed. Far away the wagon leaves with its cotton mound as the dinner bell tolls. Lavendar is gone.

Robert rubs his eyes. Lying where the wagon was, Goat's broken guitar remains.

15. EXT. COTTON FIELD PERIPHERY — TWILIGHT

Among other weary sharecroppers Robert trudges off the field with his hoe and the fractured guitar.

A crop duster skims the dim field as Elder Hadley blesses those departing. He turns to sweat-drenched Robert, who respectfully but irreverently hands the preacher his hoe.

ROBERT (SOFTLY)

I ain't afraid like that.

Robert exits. Elder Hadley, taken aback, leaning on the hoe, watches Robert head for the shacks among the trees as we hear the kindly preacher's inner monologue.

ELDER HADLEY (V.O.)

Now, I'm a preacher—Elder Hadley, Elder J. J. Hadley. And you know the Lord called on me once, when I was out there workin' jus' like you—

16. EXT. DIRT PATH — TWILIGHT

Robert trudges with his guitar through the purplish, darkening way. Other tired workers return to their shacks, as smoke wafts about from small wood fires.

ELDER HADLEY (O.S.)

He called on me an' told me—in imagination, you know—that He wanted me to preach. I told Him I was ignorant, that folks would laugh at me. But He weighed on me so, I prayed—

Silently, a sharecropper rides a mule laden with long sacks. And a man plays a "one-string" nailed to a porch post, his little daughter, dressed in red, dancing gaily.

ELDER HADLEY (CONT.) (O.S.)

I prayed out in them Piney Woods, I prayed an' I prayed—

Robert comes upon a hog pen, where VIRGINIA TRAVIS holds an oval basin filled with water, sprinkling the dusty ground. She is a slender beauty, not yet seventeen.

ELDER HADLEY (CONT.) (O.S.)

At last a great light came down to me, an' struck me hard on the head an' the shoulder an' the breast, here an' here an' here, in imagination, like I said—

She looks up to see Robert pause. Their eyes meet.

> ELDER HADLEY (CONT.) (O.S.)
>
> An' then warmth was in around my heart. An' I felt
> the Book was there, in my heart. An' I knowed, when
> I come through it an' was endowed with the Holy
> Ghost, I didn't know nothin'.

Virginia resumes her chore, and Robert walks on.

> ELDER HADLEY (CONT.) (O.S.)
>
> But my tongue was untied, an' I'm preachin' ever
> since an' I ain't afraid. No, Robert, I ain't afraid.

Virginia gazes after Robert as he departs. A dreamlost old man
passes with his fishing pole and string of fish.

17. EXT. SHACK — NIGHTFALL

A faceless shack, dark and moribund, with wood steps missing
on the front porch. Strange dissonant twanging sounds flee from
within.

18. INT. SHACK — NIGHTFALL

The moonlit floor slants toward the far corner of the room,
where Robert sits facing the converging walls. Shirtless, his
white shirt hangs from a nearby nail.

Robert wraps Goat's ruined guitar with cord, then plucks its
strings, the box to his ear. He runs a knife down the neck and
back again, the sound like a smothered shriek.

Angelic Virginia appears outside through an open window.
Hearing the grunting guitar, she pauses, water basin on hip.

Robert waxes the guitar's four strings with a candle. Virginia steps into the doorway. Robert faces the wall.

ROBERT

So how old are you.

VIRGINIA

Sixteen.

ROBERT

Better you come in then. Tell me who you are.

VIRGINIA

I'm—I'm Virginia, Travis. From Commerce. The Abbay-Leatherman farm. I'm here with my aunt, who's grievin' some.

Robert, facing the wall, shifts in his chair picking the strings. Virginia moves closer and sets the basin down.

ROBERT

Boyfriend back home?

VIRGINIA

I don't belong to anyone personal.

ROBERT

Ain't jealous if you did.

He steals a glimpse of her; she shifts her gaze. Robert inches his chair toward her, facing the wall.

ROBERT

Y'know, I'm Robert, Robert Johnson. Robert Lonnie Johnson. One of the famous Johnson boys. Robert's me an'—an' Lonnie's from my brother.

VIRGINIA

The Lonnie Johnson your kin?

ROBERT

Brother. Distant brother.

VIRGINIA

Tommy Johnson too?

ROBERT

Cousin, mostly. But I learnt my main tricks on Son House.

VIRGINIA

Where's your mother at?

ROBERT

Charley Patton taught me how to spread my hands.

VIRGINIA

Said, where's your mama—

ROBERT

I'm good as they come. An' you a womanly stranger.

VIRGINIA

You avoidin' me.

ROBERT

Ain't avoidin' you at all.

VIRGINIA

Where's your papa?

ROBERT

Why you askin' questions, girl? They dead, all of 'em.
This room here full of 'em. Only I'm gonna get out,
same way I come. This time where I'm goin' I ain't
never comin' back.

Virginia, mystified, stands behind Robert.

VIRGINIA

Where's that?

ROBERT

Chicago.

Robert strums, softly humming. He turns to the wall.

VIRGINIA

You make them records for Mr. Speir?

ROBERT

Some. A couple. But I ain't so good as ones like Son
here, or Scrappy Black.

VIRGINIA

Then who you good as?

ROBERT

You.

He lays the guitar atop the basin.

ROBERT

You goin' with me?

His back to her, Virginia retreats. He looks over to see her pause by the door.

> VIRGINIA
>
> You ain't so good as Willie Brown, neither.

> ROBERT
>
> You goin' with me?

> VIRGINIA
>
> I think your mama now suits you better. Next time at the jook maybe you tell me who you are.

She exits.

19. EXT. FISH FRY — NIGHT

While hungry sharecroppers huddle over a skillet sizzling with catfish, four women dance in the dusty yard as their men play guitar, washboard and kazoo. Now the prancing kazoo player starts tooting hard on the spout of a rusty teapot.

Gangly T-Bone draws laughs with a goofy shimmy-she-wa-wa as Virginia approaches—then abruptly heads back to the shack.

20. INT. SHACK — NIGHT

At the door Virginia pauses midsentence.

> VIRGINIA
>
> You know maybe you can—huh.

The room is empty. On the floor is Goat's useless guitar.

21. EXT. MOON LAKE LANDSCAPE — NIGHT

Around the black crescent lake wanders solitary Robert.

22. EXT. GRAVEYARD — NIGHT

CLOSEUP of an old wooden grave marker. Each line of the marker's epitaph is crudely carved into separate slats.

GRAVE MARKER

Sunday
July 10, 1923
Peyton is no more
Age 42
Tho he was a bad man in many respects,
an yet he was a most excellent field
hand, always at his
post.
On this place for 24 years.
Except the measles an its sequence, the
injury rec'd by the mule an its sequence,
he has not lost 15 days work, I verily believe, in
the remaining 19 years. I wish we could hope for
his eternal state.

Footsteps trudge through the tall grass. Someone wearing torn trousers and high black field boots briefly blocks our view of the grave marker.

IKE ZINNERMAN, 61, takes care of the overgrown graveyard. He leans his guitar against the marker and pulls some weeds from a particular grave. He sits on its tombstone, inscribed with "Mamie Zinnerman—Good Wife," and removes his boots.

Slipping a gray sack over his shoulder, tall Ike steps to an old tree and pulls moss down from its limbs. He struggles with some moss; when he removes it, he ponders a heavy rope, its noose tangled and bunched at its dangling end.

More footsteps. Robert pauses to stare up at the rope beside him.

> IKE
>
> Got my nephew, too. Wasn't but seventeen. Was out one night an' some white boys beat 'im with an iron rod. Then laid him on the track for a train to hit. Boys went home to bed an' that was it. My nephew, he thought they were his friends; they grew up together. Y'know, you find some things in this life on earth'll make you mean.

Ike resumes gathering moss, stuffing the moss in his sack.

> IKE
>
> So if it ain't Mister Downchild.

> ROBERT
>
> What's happenin', Ike?

> IKE
>
> Same ol' shit. Workin' from can to can't for plantation scrip. Pullin' this moss so's I can fix me a bed. How 'bout yourself?

> ROBERT
>
> Oh dark to dark, treadin' the mill. Playin' gui-tar now. Been bustin' up the jooks real bad.

Ike smiles.

IKE

Heard somethin' 'bout that. You givin' up harp?

ROBERT

Givin' up everything.

IKE

'Cept the womens.

Ike stuffs the last batch of moss into his sack and walks back to the graveyard.

IKE

Best go see a conjuror. Git yourself a mojo for protection.

He grabs his guitar and sits on his wife Mamie's tombstone. Reclining in the grass, Robert watches Ike tune the guitar.

IKE

Yeah. Give some tightenin' round the neck an' shoulders. There. Huh. Says, "I'm good enough if you are."

Gently picking the guitar strings, Ike sings a gentle lament in his soft, gruff baritone, titled "Shorty George."

IKE

Lord, what's the matter now? / Can't read no letter, Lord / Don't need no letter no how. (spoken) Found ol' Nat Walker Sunday mornin', Robert. Wasn't quite dead. Rushed 'im to the doctor, but—it's dangerous livin' by yourself alone.

Ike hands his guitar to Robert, who picks the guitar, as Ike picks more weeds.

IKE

Now Mamie here was different. Even when she got to be so superannuated an' all, nothin' changed: she was like about the contrariest woman I ever did know. Thought she didn't even need to die.

ROBERT

Well, maybe she ain't down there.

IKE

Well, maybe she ain't. But I can hear her still, if I takes a notion. Mmm. Folks don't always die too fast, if you know what I mean.

Ike scoops up some grave dirt and pockets it. He sits on her tombstone as Robert keeps picking the guitar strings.

IKE

One last thing 'fore ol' Icarus call it a night. Won't be long 'til you play gui-tar good like you do harp. Then you start gettin' hot to go, all ramblified like I was. That time come, don't you lay your gui-tar down for no one, son—no man or no woman. Oh you can bet them friendly strangers'll come yo' way with their helpin' hands, folks sayin' they really found you. Now that jus' hoodoo—bunch o' lies. Ain't he or she or them or it that you belong to. Only lead you straight to Hell.

Robert sits up and watches Ike put on his boots. They have two heels each, facing in opposite directions.

IKE

Got to take care—these Piney Woods eat meat. If
later you hear footsteps, they ain't mine.

Ike trudges slowly toward the graveyard gate.

IKE

Night, son.

ROBERT

Night, Ike.

23. INT. IKE'S SHACK — NIGHT

From within the eerie darkness we see Ike arrive. He leans his
guitar against the wall, sits on his bed to remove his boots, and
quietly prays.

IKE (LOW)

The Lord's my shepherd, I don't want nothin'. He sets
me down in green fields, He lead me to the river an'
He rest my soul—

Ike stuffs his mattress with moss. Then he takes off his clothes,
sneaks a hit of hootch and gets into bed.

IKE (LOW)

I don't fear no evil 'cause You with me, Lord. Mmm.
All right.

Ike falls asleep. Then, inexplicably, the sound of random picking
of his guitar strings. He sits up. The room is still.

IKE (LOW)

Thou anoint my head with oil, my cup run over.
Goodness an' mercy'll follow me all my days, an' I
be dwellin' in the Lord's house forever. Amen. Okay.

Ike reclines, the guitar plays again. He sits up, the playing stops.
He looks around.

IKE (LOW)

That you, Mamie? Huh? You forget what things is
like down here? Hush up so's I can get my rest. I ain't
been playin' none o' them blues, so don't you worry—

The guitar falls over with a crash. Ike jumps to his feet.

IKE (LOW)

Now I's gettin' right smart. You listen up. I been
good, leadin' a clean an' humble life, an' I don't need
you remindin' me how fearful an' lonesome things
here really is. So lay off woman 'fore I—*damn*.

More shrill now, the strings are picked higher up the guitar neck.
Ike grabs the guitar by the neck and squeezes hard.

IKE (LOW)

You hear me, Mamie? I warned you. I warned you,
girl. Jus' remember you still my wife. You hear me?
Huh? Mamie?

He pauses and looks around nervously.

IKE (LOW)

That you, Mamie? Or maybe, someone else—

He reaches for his clothes.

IKE (LOW)

Sweet Jesus. Oh, no. Oh, Lord—

Ike dresses, grabs the guitar and heads out the door.

IKE (LOW)

I swear. I swear, Mamie. I swear, darlin'—

24. EXT. GRAVEYARD — NIGHT

Asleep, Robert hears Ike's footsteps and wakens. Frightened Ike trudges over to him and, trembling, hands him his guitar.

IKE

Can't play no more, gave my wife my word I won't.

ROBERT

But—

Insistently Ike puts the guitar in Robert's hand.

IKE

Take care what you do with her.

ROBERT

Sure will, Ike.

IKE

You still callin' me that.

ROBERT

Icarus.

IKE

Like in the Bible.

He exits the graveyard. Robert remains, his back against Mamie's tombstone, searchingly picking the guitar strings.

25. EXT. GRAVEYARD — MORNING

Robert still sits against the tombstone, strumming furiously. As he hoots and hollers, a panel truck picking up migrant field hands stops on the nearby gravel road.

> TRUCK DRIVER
>
> Sixty-one! Dockery, Klein farms! Clarksdale-Greenwood!

> FIELD HANDS
>
> Say, hey! Charley Patton! Miss Lookin' Good!

> ROBERT
>
> Oh, kiss my ass!

> FIELD HAND
>
> You wish I would!

Laughter and wolf whistles as Robert walks to the truck.

26. EXT. GREENWOOD — AFTERNOON

Robert strolls down the black quarter's main street, picking and strumming his guitar. Fifty yards ahead, a rowdy mob kicks up dust. While entering a bar, Robert hears a preacher's gruff voice bellow.

> CHARLEY PATTON
>
> O Lord, give Thy servant the wisdom of the owl! Connect his spirit to the gospel telephone in the

central skies! Lighten his brow with the sun of heaven, poison his mind with love for the people! Turpentine his imagination, then grease his lips with possum oil!

27. INT. GREENWOOD BAR — AFTERNOON

Leaning on the bar, Robert jaws with the BARTENDER.

ROBERT

You put up some o' that Koo-Koo hootch I fill this place up no time. I'll play out front an' then you see.

BARTENDER

That's Charley Patton out there. Bertha Lee, Henry Sims playin' side.

ROBERT

Listen up, fish lips—I'm here to headcut that sonofabitch.

In a far corner a spidery, wizened little man wearing a fedora and shades sits with a whiskey bottle. He laughs to himself, savoring some secret, evil glee, drinking hard.

BARTENDER

Oh yeah?

ROBERT

You see.

BARTENDER

That's *Charley Patton* outside—

28. EXT. GREENWOOD — AFTERNOON

In an oversized suit and crooked bow tie, demonic little CHARLEY PATTON, 40, plays wildly to the mob with buxom BERTHA LEE and sullen Henry Sims. Charley is a bizarre hybrid with a Choctaw's light copper skin, an African's facial features, and a white man's blue eyes and wavy blond hair.

His nonstop movements are unpredictable and lewd. Singing "Shake It and Break It" like a wounded bear, he heaves his guitar up, catches it behind his back, then runs it between his legs.

> CHARLEY
>
> *You-can-shake-it-you-can-break-it-you-can-hang-it-on-the-wall / But I don' wanna catch it 'fore it fall—*

Bertha Lee wears a cowbell hanging from her neck as she boogies about and tries to keep time on tambourine. Shy Sims plays a strident violin made from a cigar box.

> CHARLEY
>
> *My jelly, my roll, sweet mama, don't you let it fall—*

Charley prances while singing, beating on his partners. The drunken, antic crowd loves it. His partners don't.

> CHARLEY
>
> *You-can-scratch-it-you-can-grab-it-you-can-break-it-you-can-twist-it / Anyways I loves to git it, I / Had I my right mind, I be worried sometime—*

The mob swells with whites and blacks, dogs and mules. Charley confronts a woman with his pelvis as Henry dips between them and Bertha Lee rings her bell.

Robert pauses in the doorway to mumble bravely to himself.

ROBERT

Okay then.

The spidery little guy holds his laughter as Robert steps toward Charley, nervously eyeing his prey, ready to pounce.

CHARLEY

I ain't got nobody here but me an' myself I / I stay blue all the time, aw, when the sun goes down / My jelly, my roll, sweet mama don' you let it fall—

While Charley humps a porch post, the spidery guy whispers in his ear, nodding toward Robert.

Instantly Charley twists around and jumps into Robert's face, pummeling him with song, forcing him back.

CHARLEY

You-can't-suck-it-you-can't-fuck-it-you-can't-poke-it-you-can't-stroke-it / Only 'cause you choked an' broke it / You choked an' broke it, boy, you choked an' broke it—

Robert is humiliated by Charley's pumping pelvis. He backs away to escape further embarrassment.

CHARLEY

Yo' jelly, yo' roll, yo' mama gonna let it fall—

Robert leaves as quickly as possible. Up the street he stops a man with a guitar and asks him something, to which he responds by pointing and sending Robert on his way.

29. INT. CONJUROR'S LOBBY — LATE AFTERNOON

A dingy lobby with folding chairs, a dead potted palm, and a sign over a counter that reads "Grinding." As a fat old woman sharpens a knife, downcast Robert enters, checks his pocket change and passes through a curtained portal in the rear.

30. INT. CONJUROR'S DEN — LATE AFTERNOON

In a tiny, green-curtained cubicle is a table with mason jars, animal skulls, hex objects, and a brass scale. A sign reads "Navigare necesse est. Vivare no est necesse."

The kindly CONJUROR, in jacket and tie, sees Robert peek in.

> ROBERT
>
> Afternoon. You the conjuror here?

> CONJUROR
>
> What is it, sonny, love or money?

> ROBERT
>
> That, too. But first I needs some help with my guitarmanship.

> CONJUROR
>
> I see, a bit more earnin' power. No problem. Come put yo' hands up so's I can weigh 'em.

Robert has his hands weighed on the shiny scale.

> CONJUROR
>
> Mmm, all right, we got ourselves a situation. You baptized, boy?

> ROBERT
>
> So I been told.

Now grave in tone and manner, the conjuror makes sure the doorway's curtains are drawn, then lowers his voice.

CONJUROR (LOW)

Well, you ain't gonna be saved by no blood of the lamb. Understand? Young man, you see what no one sees an' feel what no one feels, an' 'less you get what's inside you out, it'll *kill* you. You got the power of the hidden way—so you need a good strong hand, an' I got the one that's 'specially for you.

He displays a silvery dime affixed to a chain.

CONJUROR

Goes on the left ankle. Wear it wherever you are, there be no trouble—guaranteed. So now who's the li'l fairo that will not let you be?

ROBERT

Brownskin, name's Virginia.

CONJUROR

Old situations need old medicines. Like the song says, "Don't you worry." Put yo' hands up like so an' she be crawlin' back 'fore you say "Lemon Jefferson." Mmm. Right. Need a mojo. A "John Concubine"—

He eyes Robert's palms, puts a cloth swatch on the table, dips his fingers into jars labeled "Bone" and "Bird Parts," then sprinkles the powder on the swatch. He folds it, runs a string through the knotted ends and hands the mojo over.

CONJUROR

Now jus' say "Lemon Jefferson," she come right back.
But if he call on you 'fore she do, you listen an' don't
say nothin.'

ROBERT

If who call on me.

CONJUROR

Mr. Jefferson.

ROBERT

But, Blind Lemon dead an' gone. How he gonna do
that?

CONJUROR

His way. You play it like you live, son. But first you
listen.

31. EXT. NEAR REX THEATER — TWILIGHT

Guitar in hand, examining his new mojo, tired Robert empties
a pint of whisky on a deserted street corner.

Spotting the REX THEATER FOR COLORED PEOPLE, he
walks to the converted garage where a poster reads "THE
PAINTED DESERT" starring "Wm. Boyd—C. Gable."

The mangy little stranger from the bar sees Robert pay his nickel
admission and enter the primitive movie house.

32. INT. REX THEATER — DARK

Robert clumsily makes his way to a second-row bench in the empty garage. The chamber flickers with the black and white film.

The spidery little guy enters with bottle in hand and slides along the second row to wide-eyed Robert's side.

Still wearing his hat and shades, the stranger beholds the flickering screen. He takes a huge hit of whiskey and passes it to transfixed Robert, who takes a swig and lowers it.

> ROBERT (LOW)
>
> You ain't come for no cowboys.

> DEVILMAN (LOW)
>
> Hell no. 'Cause—

The wiry little guy, gazing through his shades at the dazzling screen, leans toward Robert as William Boyd draws his gun on-screen and aims it at him.

> DEVILMAN (HUSHED)
>
> 'Cause I'm blue, I'm black, an' I never did make myself.

Robert hands the bottle back, stealing a glimpse of him.

> ROBERT (HUSHED)
>
> You a devilman.

> DEVILMAN (HUSHED)
>
> You jus' call me . . . Dutch Boy. I seen you night an' day, man, heard you playin' far away an'—*I give a damn.*

The devilman touches his shades and grimaces. He leans toward Robert, who blinks his bloodshot eyes to stay awake.

> DEVILMAN (HUSHED)
>
> I go a ways down Charlie's Trace, 'round midnight. You git there ten minutes shy so you know you there. You go to where a road crosses that way, where a crossroads is, with yo' gui-tar you git there. I walk up, take yo' gui-tar, tune it up an' give it back, after I play it. Then you go make any ol' tangled-up song you want, don't care what.

Drunken Robert nods, nodding out. The devilman removes his shades; as he wipes them on his shirt, we see two blind eyes white with cataracts. He puts the shades back on and enjoys the movie. Sinking into a dream, Robert's eyelids flutter.

MOVIE IMAGE: Young Clark Gable dismounts and ponders his reflection in a dark stream.

> DEVILMAN (V.O.)
>
> Midnight.

DISSOLVE TO

33. INT. OLD WEST OPERA HOUSE — NIGHT

An Old West opera house filled with rowdy Delta black men and women. Amid a confusion of people onstage, an ANNOUNCER wearing top hat and tails shouts through a bullhorn.

> ANNOUNCER
>
> Brothers! Sisters! Performin' for us tonight—Blind Lemon Jefferson!

Loud cheers as a spotlight falls on rotund BLIND LEMON JEFFERSON, led onstage in a bathrobe. Abruptly his guitar is grabbed and robe removed. His fat body sparkles with sweat.

> VOICES
>
> Blind Lemon! Blind Lemon moan!

A second fat black man suddenly barrels into Lemon amid the pandemonium. The stage clears with Lemon flailing under his similarly blind foe before frantically crawling away.

Neither blind man knows where the other is. The spotlight chases them as coins shower the stage, and sweaty Lemon crawls to the footlights, shouting a high-pitched plea.

> BLIND LEMON
>
> Preachers, teachers, you's wrong to turn me over to Justice! I never been a Christian! My folk sing under torture! I sincerely don't know none o' them laws! I ain't you! It's just that I ain't feelin' so good, this not bein' my home—

DISSOLVE TO

> DEVILMAN (V.O.)
>
> You git there.

34. INT. MOVIE HOUSE — DARK

Solitary Robert wakens. He eyes the empty space beside him and remembers the devilman. He also remembers the dream.

35. EXT. CHARLIE'S TRACE — MIDNIGHT

An old handmade road sign reads "CHARLIE'S TRACE."

The camera moves down the ghostly swath through a cotton-field. Anonymous black men walk or wait on either side.

At a barren, lightless crossroads we find Robert Johnson, picking his guitar nervously, his strings out of tune.

Footsteps. Slowly they stumble forth. It's the devilman. He tips his hat, briefly revealing an old souvenir Confederate army cap underneath it that reads "FORGET? HELL!"

Without looking at Robert he takes his guitar, tunes it, turns and plays an astounding guitar part that sounds and resounds like an electric guitar. Then he hands it back and turns to go but pauses, looking Robert in the eye.

> DEVILMAN
>
> I's so broke, can't even buy my dick a doughnut.

Robert fishes in his pocket and flips him a dime that's fumbled and lands in the dirt. The devilman picks it up, tips his hat, then stumbles off into the night.

> DEVILMAN
>
> Talk some shit, man, talk some shit.

Robert falls down on his knees at the crossroads, strumming a fierce guitar riff as the devilman's words fade.

> DEVILMAN
>
> Won't nothin' be the same no more—won't nothin'
> be the same.

DISSOLVE TO

36. INT. JOOK JOINT — NIGHT

SILENT IMAGE: In a dim jook somewhere in the Delta, a chaos of dancers, none recognizable. Two seated youths sing and play guitars. One pinches his nostrils while laughing and singing. His partner skims a bone across his strings.

Robert, dirty and unkempt, tired, sits by the musicians. His furtive eyes never stray from their hands.

DISSOLVE TO

37. INT. BARRELHOUSE — NIGHT

SILENT IMAGE: Robert, more unkempt, sits in a jammed roadside shanty swigging whiskey while studying a barrelhouse piano and vocal performance by a young woman.

A painted wench puts her arm around Robert, then rubs her breast on his elbow. He doesn't blink. She licks his ear.

DISSOLVE TO

38. EXT. LEVEE TENT — LATE NIGHT

SILENT IMAGE: Kerosene lamps hang from a canopy as brawny levee workers bump and grind with their female visitors from town. A young man pounding a snare drum drives the beat as an old-timer hoots and blows on a fife.

Robert sits alone by the Mississippi River, writing in a small black book.

A soused worker carries his girl to the river and dumps her in. She staggers ashore and embraces him.

Robert looks on. Haggard almost beyond recognition, he slings his guitar onto his back and heads off.

39. EXT. COTTON FIELDS — DAY

A truck rumbles in noisily from the distant levee; as it chugs by we see Robert in back, asleep with his guitar.

40. INT. JOOK JOINT — NIGHT

The musicians and random percussionists keep the dance rhythm hot as Son introduces a new blues.

> SON
>
> This one's on me, just as well admit it! This is the truth! 'Course, some of it's a little addition, but the biggest of it's the truth, 'cause I'm a preacher! 'Least I was 'fore I started this junk!

> WILLIE
>
> Lord have mercy!

> SON
>
> *Gonna get me religion, gonna join the Baptist Church / Gonna be a Baptist preacher so I sure won't have to work—*

Guitar on his back, Robert eyes the musicians from the doorway. Son sings as surprised Willie eyes Robert back.

> SON
>
> *Well, I met the blues this mornin', walkin' jus' like a man—*

> WILLIE
>
> Say, Son!

SON

Said, "Good mornin', Blues, give me yo' right hand—"

WILLIE

Son! Look who's come in the door!

Robert works his way through the dancing crowd.

SON

Whoa, it's Little Robert—

WILLIE

An' he got hisself a gui-tar!

The bluesmen laugh hard while straining to sustain their performance. Grim Robert, weary and worn, confronts them with a steady glare.

SON

Well, boy, you got that gui-tar now—what you do with that thing?

WILLIE

You can't do nothin' with it!

The guitar playing ensues as Robert keeps glaring at Son.

ROBERT

Well, I'll tell you what.

SON

What's that.

ROBERT

Let me take your seat a minute.

>   WILLIE

Hooo-boy!

>   ROBERT

Said I'm takin' yo' seat, Son.

>   SON

All right, for a minute, an' you better do somethin'
with it—

In the frenzy, Son stands and winks at Willie. Robert sits as Son
exits, and Willie follows him toward the door. There, overcome
with laughter, Son and Willie meet and drink up.

>   SON

You seen that boy's face?

>   WILLIE

'Bout turned black as a ghost when you give it!

Suddenly STUNNING GUITAR SOUNDS leap forth. Robert
plays his own "Preachin' Blues" to everyone's amazement.

>   ROBERT

*Mmmmm mmmmmm! I's up this mornin', blues
walkin' like a man / Worried blues give me yo' right
hand—*

Son and Willie turn as the camera whips back to find glimpses,
between dancers, of Robert hunched over his guitar, shouting,
body shifting to the beat.

>   SON

Say, what's that—

WILLIE

Holy shit—

ROBERT

The blues grabbed Mama's child, tore 'im all upside down / Travel on, poor Bob, jus' can't turn you 'round—

Standing amid the dancers is Virginia, staring at Robert.

ROBERT

The blues is a low-down, achin' heart disease / Like consumption, killin' me by degrees—

41. EXT. JOOK JOINT — NIGHT

Son and Willie follow Robert out of the jook.

SON

Now man ain't that somethin' fast—

WILLIE

What you talkin' 'bout that trick anyways?

Each grabs a bottle of hootch at the stand.

SON

How the hell you do it, Robert?

ROBERT

Just like you, Son. Just like you.

WILLIE

Damn, it ain't been a year ago—

Robert starts drifting off. Son catches up and walks through the crowd beside him.

> SON
>
> Now, Robert—Robert, you go 'round playin' these Saturday night balls, let me give you some instruction—

Robert ignores him, lost in another world, drinking.

> SON
>
> See you gotta be careful, 'cause you mighty wild 'bout the womens. Now when you be playin' an' they's full o' that hootch an' snuff all mixed together, an' come an' call you, "Daddy, play it again Daddy"—well, don't let it run you crazy, or—

Seeing beautiful Virginia standing off to the side with another woman, Robert leaves Son.

> SON
>
> —you liable to get killed.

Robert and Virginia face each other. He takes her hand. Son watches them with Willie.

> WILLIE
>
> Little Robert. Huh.

Robert leads Virginia away.

> SON
>
> He's gone now.

42. **EXT. FIELD NEAR HERCULES' SHACK — LATE NIGHT**

Robert and Virginia walk hand in hand toward the festive, glowing shack. They pause to gaze into each other's eyes.

> ROBERT
>
> You goin' with me?

> VIRGINIA
>
> I don't know nothin' about you, Robert. But I know who you are.

Tenderly they kiss. Then they head for the shack.

> VIRGINIA
>
> When a man goes down his road, he goes with a friend.

43. **INT. HERCULES' SHACK — LATE NIGHT**

A noisy house party in a sparsely furnished shack. More wild dancing, this time to Sidney Bechet's "Preaching Blues," a rocking 1931 recording played on a Victrola.

Twanging a washtub bass, Robert's stout half-sister HERCULES spots him walking in.

> HERCULES
>
> You calls it a garbage can, I calls it a streamline bass!

She rushes over to Robert and makes him dance.

> HERCULES
>
> Well, my oh my, Robert Dusty! Now don't jus' stand there—shake that thing!

They dance spectacularly to the scintillating swing rhythm as her husband GRANVILLE greets Virginia. Robert keeps an eye on his guitar while Hercules spins him.

> HERCULES
>
> Baby brother's lookin' good!

> ROBERT
>
> Hey, easy on me, Hercules!

> HERCULES
>
> So fine seein' yo' sweet face again! Now who you with—somethin' special?

Robert grins sheepishly.

> HERCULES
>
> Whoa, Robert—shake it, man!

44. **EXT. PORCH — LATE NIGHT**

Through the screen door we see Hercules lead Virginia away. Granville and Robert sit down on opposite swinging loveseats. Robert tunes his guitar as they talk.

> GRANVILLE
>
> Say, Robert, if you don't mind me askin', that angel chile you with—

> ROBERT
>
> Yeah, she gonna be with me a while.

> GRANVILLE
>
> Lord, Lord—li'l girl's a livin' doll. But I can see she gonna need a whole lot o' providin'—what all the womens gotta have, y'know.

ROBERT

Aw, that ain't what they gotta have.

GRANVILLE

Well, what I'm sayin' is, you best be helpin' out the Big Boss more.

ROBERT

Naw, I don't do that.

GRANVILLE

What you mean you "don't do that"? Gotta live somehow. Gotta eat. An' if you gonna be providin' for—

ROBERT

Ain't providin' for no bossman no more, neither.

GRANVILLE

Well, like the Good Book say—

ROBERT

God makes man, man makes money.

GRANVILLE

You reaps what you done sowed.

ROBERT

An' you don't trust a soul.

GRANVILLE

Well, you gotta work for someone.

ROBERT

I'm makin' my resolution. I'll work for that.

GRANVILLE

That's it, you tell me now. I'm listenin'—

ROBERT

I'm puttin' out a prayer, in the mornin'. I'm gonna tell the Lord to search my heart, an' if He finds anything hangin' there like a double shovel, a gang plow, a cotton sack, a mule, I want Him to move it, an' cast it into the Sea of Forgiveness, so it won't rise against me in this world either the world to come.

GRANVILLE

Huh, now wait—

ROBERT

Your soul, it reaps less from knowin' a little gain than losin' a whole lot more, I reckon.

GRANVILLE

Then boy, you goin' to Hell.

ROBERT

Hell ain't where you dead, man. It's where you alive.

45. INT. HERCULES' KITCHEN — LATE NIGHT

Goat enters and puts down a can labeled "STERNO / Cooking Fuel" as the Victrola plays. He takes a rag and matches, then bites the can's lid off with his teeth.

Robert enters. Goat, his bloody hare's foot around his neck, prepares his poisonous drink.

GOAT

This canned heat'll get yo' gui-tar singin' like it
should, 'cause *mmm!* you gotta be open up 'fore you
can do any kind o' work. The openin's what makes
you one of us—

Robert sees him pour the red fuel into the rag, wring the liquid
into another can, grab a sugar jar and two tin cups.

GOAT

Sugar . . . water, the way you like it . . . there. Mmm,
all right.

He fills one cup, tastes it approvingly, then fills the second for
Robert. They exit via the kitchen door.

46. EXT. HERCULES' SHACK — LATE NIGHT

Goat imparts some wisdom to Robert en route to the road.

GOAT

Now see, whenever you run up on somethin' playin',
y'know yo' changes like it's connectin' somethin'
together, y'know how to hold it—

SAM (O.S.)

There you is—gotcha, Goat! You ain't playin'—I'll
beat yo' ass! Gonna beat yo' black ass, boy!

Robert drinks as nasty ONE-LEGGED SAM stalks them.

GOAT

—but you got to feel it an' get it, it'll mumble
through you gradually, then you knows how to run

it right. Boogies, blues, they come right to you. That's
when you make some money, at that time—

The old cuss Sam suddenly tackles Goat, slamming him down.
Sam beats on Goat, who's too drunk to resist, rolling toward
the side door.

> SAM
>
> You play now 'fore I wipe my nose all over you, you
> drunken nigger!

The revelers rush out. Robert jumps on Sam's back as Sam tries
to twist Goat's head off. Goat bites Sam's fingers.

Robert bites Sam's peg leg, then yanks it and rips it off. Hercules
grabs the leg and clubs Sam mercilessly.

Sam lies twitching and bleeding on the ground. Hercules returns
the prosthetic to Robert, who glares at Sam, then heaves the leg
into the dark field.

47. INT. HERCULES' SHACK — WEE HOURS

Everyone is sprawled about the candlelit floor. A drowsy couple
has a drunken exchange.

> HUSBAND (LOW)
>
> I'm proud o' you, darlin'.

> WIFE (LOW)
>
> I'm tired o' you, too, babe.

When Granville stirs, Robert lulls him to sleep by quoting the
Bible while moving to Virginia, dozing beside Hercules.

> ROBERT (LOW)

An' the Lord make the earth empty, an' make it waste, an' turn it upside down, scatter its childrens all 'round the town, fuck an' kill each other—

> GRANVILLE (ASLEEP)

'Cause the Lord has spoke the word. The earth mourns an' fades away. The earth fades—

Robert kneels by Virginia. Slowly she wakens, mystified.

> VIRGINIA (LOW)

I was dreamin', Robert. Dreamin' I was dreamin' I was with a tiny child, not a boy an' not a girl, we was sleepin' somewhere. 'Twas dark but we knew where we was—

> ROBERT (LOW)

C'mon, let's go.

She takes his hand, they exit. The others remain on the floor, fetal, sleeping like infants.

48. EXT. LEVEE SLOPE — WEE HOURS

Moonlit Virginia lies naked on the moist, sloping turf. Robert kneels naked beside her. Gracefully she rolls on top of him, kissing his slender body, as he kisses hers.

49. EXT. LEVEE — BEFORE DAWN

The levee swells up from the backwater flatlands like an awesome monolith. Leaning against the purple predawn sky, the

flood wall seems to prevent the very sun from rising. Crickets
punctuate the dark stillness.

The figures of Robert and Virginia trek distantly atop the levee.
The camera tracks left to right with them.

> VIRGINIA
>
> You been to Alabama, Robert?

> ROBERT
>
> Bad place for musicianers. Can't be hangin' 'round
> no dead folk.

> VIRGINIA
>
> You been there?

> ROBERT
>
> No.

> VIRGINIA
>
> Well, it's beautiful, nothin' like Mississippi at all.
> There's a fine big stretch where I was born at Red
> Bay—people hear things there, fearful things, like
> angels moanin' an' bells tollin' when there ain't none.
> Sometimes they seen lost souls flyin' o'er the bay to
> an island of light. That's what they say. I seen a whole
> lotta bones turn up in the fields. There was an open
> passage I remember once, goin' down under the field,
> an' me an' two girls went in. Saw the ashes from the
> fires that the slaves used to make. The passage is
> closed now.

Robert and Virginia pause on the elevated gravel road. Panning
360 degrees around the dim landscape, we see the river, the black
cypress swamps, the levee road stretching out ahead, the slum-
bering fields and shacks.

ROBERT

I'm gonna show you a whole other world, places
where slaves never been.

He bends low and picks up a stone, then tosses it out over the
sullen swamp toward a distant splash.

ROBERT

Ain't no family, ain't no friends, ain't nothin' here
to keep us.

Taking Virginia's hand, he leads her homeward.

ROBERT

Kansas City's out there, an' St. Louis, an' y'know
Chicago ain't that far. They got all kinds of
instruments or parts you want up there from slides to
strings, all made of steel. Blind Blake, Scrappy Black
an' a whole lot of 'em, Lou Armstrong is there. They
bug the music, make you play, see who can cut who.
That's why you get good, y'know—

They fade into the dimness. We remain, staring at the swamp, as
somewhere a rooster crows. A little sign in the foreground reads:
"Night Travel on Levee Prohibited."

FADE OUT.

50. INT. HERCULES' SHACK — DAY

On a gray, gloomy day, Robert leaves an inner bedroom as the
radio announces a Fourth of July sale in Clarksdale. Suspended
on the far wall, a plain white bridal dress and veil.

Moving into the main room, Robert sits by the Victrola with
guitar and hootch, listening to Skip James's haunting "Devil Got

My Woman," quietly humming with the falsetto voice. Reclined on the sofa, Virginia rests, in discomfort.

> VICTROLA
>
> *I'd rather be the Devil, than to be that woman's man—*

Concentrating hard, Robert quietly hums along. Virginia rests behind him on the sofa, a wet cloth cooling her brow.

A strange rumbling and sputtering sound emerges outside. Through a window we see Goat drive a jalopy, with rags on its wheels instead of tires, up to the shack.

With brow furrowed, Robert listens to the Victrola as Goat enters and approaches Robert with a small book.

> GOAT
>
> Need a bag.

Robert points to the kitchen, where Goat goes. He reappears with a brown paper bag, leaves the book by Robert and exits. The book is titled *Exegesis of Musical Knowledge*.

Through the window Goat is seen lifting the car's hood. He reaches down with the bag, then straightens up with the bag soaked in oil. He reenters the shack.

> GOAT
>
> Back a minute.

He returns to the kitchen. Seconds later, smoke drifts out. Goat comes back with two jars filled with a black liquid. He and Robert drink up.

ROBERT

Where's the car from?

GOAT

Jackson. Got it with the six bucks for my rights. The book there, too.

VICTROLA

Aw, nothin' but the Devil changed my baby's mind—

GOAT

Can't read it, but it's good to have. It's a book. Tells you yo' bass strings from them sopranos.

Through the window Lavendar is seen towing One-Legged Sam in her strange wooden wagon. She drinks from an oil can while limping down the dirt road.

Granville enters with his elderly friend JACK OWENS, as Robert drinks his brew and drunken Goat dashes outside after Lavendar.

GRANVILLE

Afternoon! Like that Skip James you got there. Jack Owens here's from Bentonia, up the hills like Skip—

Her hair pinned and wearing shades, Hercules sits with Virginia, feeling her forehead while the Victrola plays.

JACK

Yes, uh-huh, I knows Skippy a bit. I learnt that boy a few things, uh-huh—

Outside we see Goat fall down while cranking his car as Hercules, examining Virginia, seems alarmed. She grabs Robert by the collar and hauls him into the kitchen.

>   HERCULES
>
> Come on, boy, 'bout time you growed up. An' I'll
> make sure you do—

>   JACK
>
> Mmm. "Devil Got My Woman." That's Skippy, uh-
> huh, good tune there—

51. INT. KITCHEN — DAY

Bursting into the kitchen, throwing her bulk around, she
bounces Robert about the small room, scolding him.

>   HERCULES
>
> So who you think you are, baby brother? Who you
> think you are, stayin' out all night in them jooks,
> comin' home lookin' like a fright all filthy—huh?
> Why you beatin' up on Jesus so? Tell me!

>   ROBERT (MUTTERING)
>
> Reven—

>   HERCULES
>
> An' how 'bout Virginia? Po' chile alone on that sofa
> now suffering! Huh? She yo' wife or ain't she? You
> married, boy, or how come?

>   ROBERT (MUTTERING)
>
> How co—

Hercules slaps drunken Robert and pins him to the wall.

>   HERCULES
>
> You sober up! You quit that devil music, go out
> in that field pick cotton like a *man*! Can't you see

she gonna need your help? Don't you know what's
happenin'? Can't you tell?

ROBERT

What, she bein' sick an' such—

HERCULES

Sick? You think she's like on her back with fever? That
girl, she's carryin' your child, man! 'Ginia's pregnant,
Robert! You gonna be a *father* soon—

Stupefied Robert is shaken quick.

52. INT. HERCULES' SHACK — AFTERNOON

He sits on the sofa, laying a wet rag on Virginia's brow.

53. EXT. PORCH — AFTERNOON

Jack and Granville sit on the loveseats. As a little boy watches
Granville make him a guitar with fishing line and a cigar box,
the older man talks to the boy at his feet.

GRANVILLE

Little boys have to be careful, they can be so triflin'
sometimes. In Africa they gets punished when they
been bad, folks put 'em on the banjo, that's in yo'
grandpappy's time. When he play that night they
sing 'bout that boy, tell all 'bout 'im. That's "puttin'
on the banjo," an' that boy sure better change his
ways—

Old Jack shouts out a riveting version of Skip James's song.

JACK

*Ohhh, it must be the Devil, baby, to be that woman's
hoooooo—*

DISSOLVE TO

54. EXT. FOREST — NIGHT

In a clearing, Robert, his guitar leaning against a tree and his black book upside down, paces in the shadows pensively.

> JACK (O.S.) (CONT.)
>
> *Ohhhh, it must be the Devil, baby, done change that woman's miiiiind—*

DISSOLVE TO

55. EXT. COTTON FIELD — NOON

Serious and steadfast, Robert chops and chops in the brutal heat with his hoe. Beside him, Granville lustily stuffs his long sack with cotton.

Elder Hadley strolls by in a red sports jacket, tipping his hat and smiling at Robert, who chops harder.

> JACK (O.S.) (CONT.)
>
> *Oh, the Devil got religion, baby, but he joined no Baptist church—*

DISSOLVE TO

56. INT. BEDROOM — MIDNIGHT

Robert sleeps under moonlit sheets with his pregnant wife. He opens one eye, then rises and sits on the edge of the bed, gazing out the black window.

Through the window, an old tree trembles in the gusty night.

FADE OUT.

FADE IN TO

57. EXT. HERCULES' SHACK — MORNING

Hercules, Granville, Robert and Virginia, dressed in their Sunday best, walk under the tree and climb into Granville's old Model-T. The car chugs and sputters away.

58. EXT. CHURCH — MORNING

A white church on a little hill, shaded by a chinaberry tree. As congregants sing "Choose Your Seat and Set Down" before the service, Granville's car parks on the side.

> SINGING
>
> *Ohhh, Lordy, jus' give me a long white robe, in the heaven / Choose yo' seat an' set down—*

Hercules and Granville greet REVEREND GATES at the door as Robert helps Virginia out of the car. Robert is impeccably groomed in hat, suit with suspenders, white shirt and tie. Arm in arm they approach the smiling preacher.

> GATES
>
> God willing, won't be long now— you as big as can be, chile!

> VIRGINIA
>
> You know, Reverend Gates, I been feelin' like there's miracles in secret all around me now—

> GATES
>
> That's 'cause you're lookin' for Deliverance, Mrs. Johnson! But to win Deliverance, you got to wait on

the movements of Providence—good mornin' Mr. Johnson, nice seein' you again—

Robert and Virginia enter the church.

SINGING

Trouble over, choose yo' seat an' set down—

59. INT. CHURCH — MORNING

The pews are filled with congregants in song. Hercules leads Granville to a seat up front.

SINGING

Ohhhhh, Jesus, was my mother there? / In the heaven, choose yo' seat an' set down, trouble over—

The sublime singing dissipates while Robert and Virginia slip into seats beside Hercules and Granville.

The entire pulpit is covered with white sheets. The powerful voice of Reverend Gates bellows above a few fading singers. Congregants' responses are noted in parentheses.

GATES

Now chillun, I gonna speak the truth—I'm goin' if it takes my life! (Amen!) I don't care what the world may say, I'm goin'! (Yessuh!) We have a whole lotta peoples round here, ohhhh, haven't connected themselves to no church! (Tell it! Truth!) An' lotsa people 'round here sayin' they been borned again—but there ain't no church around 'em! (Yessuh! Tell it!)

CALLETTA CRAFT, a curvaceous woman of thirty-five who sits with her two young sons, swoons over a spiritual threshold into a lilting, cooing response.

GATES

So I'm in doubt 'bout yo' REGENERATION! (Tell it!)

The lilting voice strengthens as a deeper male voice intones.

GATES

YOU AIN'T SHOWED AS MUCHA SENSE AS THOSE LITTLE OL' MICE! Why I can remember one mornin' I walked into the kitchen an' saw a mouse with a CRUMB in his mouth—

Virginia hums fervently as Robert skims the hymnal. The room starts reeling hypnotically, led by Calletta and Granville.

GATES

SO I RUSHED THE LITTLE OL' MOUSE!

CONGREGATION

Ohhhhhhhh yeahhhhhhhhh—

GATES

An' he tried to get through that hole an' carry the little crumb with 'im! When I kep' a-rushin' at 'im, HE THROWED THE CRUMB AWAY AN' SAVED HIS LIFE!

CONGREGATION

Ohhhhhhhh, we gonna see Himmmmmmm—

GATES

Now there's a whole lotta workin' mens an' womens 'round here tryin' to hold onto their little crumbs but GOD'LL THROW 'EM AWAY! AN' GO TO HEAVEN WITHOUT 'EM! (Amen!)

CONGREGATION

Good, good Lord! Ohhhh, he gone!

GATES

God'll go alone, He ain't gonna wait! So throw that ol'
plantation scrip away! You gotta go if it takes yo' life!

Reverend Gates bursts into song, arms waving.

GATES

An' I'm a-goin' if it takes my life—Sing it!

GATES AND CONGREGATION

If I die on that sad ol' field, I'm goin' if it takes my life—

DISSOLVE TO

60. INT. CHURCH — TWILIGHT

Reverend Gates chants with an urgent, dark growl. An almost
sinister tone in his hypnotic voice and delivery.

Robert and Virginia mouth silent chants, kneeling at a front
bench. Older congregants crowd them in the delirium.

GATES

Oh-when-them-Roman-soldiers-come-riding-in-
full-speed-an'-plunged-Him-in-the-side-ohhh!
Almighty-said-the-water's-for-baptism-an'-the-
blood's-for-cleansin'. I-don't-care-how-MEAN-you-
been, God's-almighty-blood-will-cleanse-you,
great-God-will-come—

Virginia perspires profusely. The throng closes in. Women moan
and shriek. Eyes closed, knees bent, body limp, Calletta is entranced. The room is possessed.

VOICES

Goin' through! God fly! Holy dance!

DEACON

HOLY DANCE!

GATES

They-set-to-look-about-the-temple, Jesus-said-to-tear-it-down-an'-in-three-days-I'll-ride-up-again. He-was talkin'-'bout-His-templed-body-hangin'-there-bleedin'-there—

Eyelids fluttering, Calletta undulates with sensual abandon. Softly, lost in the din, she mutters her signal while moving toward Robert with eyes closed, lips moist.

CALLETTA (LOW)

Oh movin' . . . oh, under, oh, papa . . . I'm goin', oh God—

As others lapse into trance, Calletta kneels before Robert, leaning back, arms outstretched, breasts heaving.

GATES

But-they-didn't-know-what-He-was-talkin'-'bout, I-seen-while-He-was-hangin'-them-mountings-begin-to-tremble-that-Jesus-was-ridin'-on, His-blood-was-droppin'-down-the-mounting, holy-blood-was-dropping-down—

Virginia, sweating terribly, cringing, chants silently as Robert beholds Calletta.

> GATES

Our-Maker-was-a'dyin', the-Creator-of-the-sun-
OHHH-OOOOOO! He-make-the-MOON—

61. EXT. CHURCH — NIGHTFALL

The service is over. Cooing sighs persist inside as dazed congregants exit past a CONJUROR under a tattered awning, his para-
phernalia on display, softly calling.

> CONJUROR (LOW)

Good with two magics better than one . . . Good
with two magics better than one . . . Good with two
magics—

Hercules and Granville walk to the Model T. Robert, holding
Virginia, follows. After they get in the car it sputters away, down-
hill, headlights bouncing.

62. INT. MODEL T — NIGHT

Granville drives while singing a responsive duet with Hercules
in the front seat.

> HERCULES

Ohhhhh, Lordy, jus' give me a long white robe—

> GRANVILLE

In the heaven—

> HERCULES

Choose yo' seat an' set down—

> GRANVILLE

Trouble over—

Behind them, Virginia lies with her head on Robert's lap.

> VIRGINIA (WEAK)
>
> Robert—

Robert stares out the window. Virginia is in obvious distress, perspiring heavily and getting faint.

> VIRGINIA (WEAK)
>
> Robert—

> ROBERT
>
> What's happenin', Virginia?

> GRANVILLE
>
> I'm throwin' them crumbs away!

> HERCULES
>
> Tell it!

> VIRGINIA (WEAK)
>
> Robert, get me to the doctor—

> GRANVILLE
>
> Robert!

> HERCULES
>
> *Ohhhhh, Jesus! Was my mother there?*

> ROBERT
>
> Granville!

> GRANVILLE
>
> Robert, I hear them say that the Devil was in Heaven one time when the people was feelin' in danger—

> ROBERT

Granville—

> GRANVILLE

—which is why the Lord put him in a sealed-up place
where he can't get—

> ROBERT

Granville, step on it—

> GRANVILLE

Say, what's goin' on back there?

Hercules turns around to find Virginia in labor.

> HERCULES

Virginia!

> ROBERT

Granville! Virginia's startin' to percolate!

> VIRGINIA (FAINT)

Oh, Robert . . . Jesus, please . . .

63. EXT. GRAVEL ROAD — NIGHT

The Model-T creeps through the rain on the pitted road.

64. INT. MODEL T — NIGHT

Moaning softly, Virginia writhes in pain as Robert pats her face
with his white kerchief.

HERCULES

Ohhh, Lordy, jus' give me a long white robe—

ROBERT

HEAR ME, GRANVILLE? 'GINIA'S PERCOLATIN'!
FAST NOW, GRANVILLE, FAST—

GRANVILLE

I heared ya! I'm goin' as fast as I can—

He steps on the gas, the engine sputters, the car stops.

GRANVILLE

Damn. Stalled out. God damn—

Robert is terrified. Virginia writhes in his lap as Granville and
Hercules get out to push. He cranks and cranks, the motor
coughs, the car rolls forward, the motor dies. They keep pushing
the car into the blackness.

VIRGINIA

Oh Robert . . . hurry . . .

Finally, a thundering car approaches from behind, then roars
past with white voices hooting and hollering, "NIGGER!"

Robert cradles Virginia as the Model T crawls onward, taking a
verse from a work song and softly singing to her.

ROBERT

*Girl, I love you, tell the world I do, hey / Girl, I love
you, tell the world I do—*

An old panel truck overtakes the Model T and pulls over.

> ROBERT
>
> *Girl, I love you, tell the world I do, heyyyy / Hope
> someday you come to love me, too—*

> VIRGINIA
>
> Oh, papa, help me—

The squinting black truck driver waddles into the headlights of
the oncoming jalopy.

65. EXT. HOSPITAL — NIGHT

The panel truck rumbles up to the small hospital. Robert hops
out, takes Virginia in his arms toward the "Colored" door.

66. INT. HOSPITAL — NIGHT

Robert paces the floor as white hospital personnel pass to and
fro. A WHITE NURSE chats with a doctor, pointing her clipboard
at Robert. Then she approaches him.

> NURSE
>
> You the husband?

> ROBERT
>
> Yes, ma'am.

> NURSE (WRITING)
>
> Occupation—

> ROBERT
>
> Farmer.

NURSE

It was a boy, Johnson. Room two-one-three upstairs.

She exits. Robert follows. She sends him back the opposite way.

67. INT. "COLORED" HOSPITAL ROOM — NIGHT

A window sprays moonlight into the dark, cluttered cell. Buckets and mops, a balance scale and two shrouded bodies on gurneys.

Robert enters and shuts the door tightly. He looks about the room, then wanders to the first gurney and peeks under the sheet. He neatly puts the stranger's sheet back in place.

He scans the room, fixing briefly on the second gurney, then shifts his gaze out the window, talking to Virginia.

ROBERT

That was good today, way you took it an' all. You the type does her cryin' on the inside. Mmm.

Distantly he gazes through his reflection on the window pane. His eyes lower, he taps his knuckles on the pane. Silence.

ROBERT

But now I ain't got patience for no problems, hear? Long as you here in Mississippi, girl, you never will get well. We got work to do, followin' that cotton 'round. I'm dressin' like a preacher so we can go from town to town—

Robert steps to the second gurney and ponders the rippled, moonlit sheets. He runs his hand over the shrouded body, withdrawing it at a melon-sized lump between the legs.

> ROBERT
>
> "Chicago." How's that sound—

His back to the moonlit window, Robert stares down at the corpse. The rippled, shadowed sheets glow eerily.

> ROBERT
>
> 'Ginia? You goin' with me?

He stiffens with fear.

> ROBERT
>
> You goin' with me?

Robert slowly pulls the shroud back, then throws himself onto the body of beautiful Virginia in a fit of sorrow. The camera pans outward to the moon.

> ROBERT (WEEPING)
>
> Don't cry, Virginia, don't cry—

DISSOLVE TO

68. EXT. DELTA LANDSCAPE — NIGHT

Below the moon the land lies sluggish, an expanse of unending blackness graced by the cypress-studded Yazoo River.

DISSOLVE TO

69. EXT. RIVERSIDE — DAY

A gloomy day. Across the river, a large crowd of mourners in a cypress grove cemetery.

DISSOLVE TO

70. EXT. GRAVEYARD — DAY

A grievous throng at Virginia's grave. Robert kneels dry-eyed as Reverend Gates pontificates with arms upraised and the gravedigger pats down dirt. Sudden tumult at graveside. Hysterical Hercules pushes mourners aside while lunging for the grave. Granville grabs her as Calletta Craft faints. Calleta is laid onto the back seat of Granville's car. Staring at her deathly visage, Robert seems disturbed.

DISSOLVE TO

71. INT. TENT — NIGHTFALL

Deacon Bates leads the stomping, shuffling mourners in a delirious "ring shout." Robert sits with his guitar on his lap in a candlelit corner. Calletta steps over and nudges her hip against Robert's shoulder. Their eyes meet, she touches his face.

DISSOLVE TO

72. INT. CALLETTA'S BEDROOM — NIGHT

Candlelit Robert and Calletta make love. Robert's pensive voice emerges over the image, followed by Calletta's. Each sounds calm, detached, isolated.

> ROBERT (V.O.)
>
> I got somethin' to say. A man, like a god, I mean, hisself, through her mouth he got her speech—

> CALLETTA (V.O.)
>
> Robert, squeeze my heart, Robert—

73. INT. CALLETTA'S BEDROOM — MIDNIGHT

Calletta sleeps as Robert, dressed neatly now, quietly bundles his belongings, grabs his guitar and exits.

> ROBERT (V.O.)
>
> An,' this voice has done me so as I'll never be my own self again, after I listened, ever since.

> CALLETTA (V.O.)
>
> Robert, love me—

74. INT. KITCHEN — MIDNIGHT

Robert scoops pomade from a tin. Facing the camera as if a mirror, he slicks his hair back until it's almost flat.

His appearance altered, Robert takes a large hit of whiskey. He stares searchingly into the camera, unblinking.

75. INT. CALLETTA'S BEDROOM — MIDNIGHT

Robert is seen through the window with guitar and bundle, swigging his bottle, marching off into the night.

Calletta wakens as his footsteps fade. Seeing she's been left alone, she rushes inside to the other rooms, then returns to the window.

Meek little ESAU stands in the doorway rubbing his eye.

> ESAU
>
> Mama, I got a wind in my belly—

76. INT. HOSPITAL ROOM — NIGHT

In the dark cell, Robert stares down at the moonlit sheet covering Virginia's corpse.

> ESAU (V.O.)
>
> I got a wind in my belly, Mama—

77. EXT. JOOK JOINT — NIGHT

A drunk squats on a stoop outside the jammed, uproarious jook, savoring a can of kerosene. As he lifts it to his lips, two JOKERS drop a lit cigarette into the fuel. The drunk flees to the woods screaming flames.

> JOKERS
>
> CHARLEY PATTON!

SUPER: Near Lula, Mississippi, 1934

78. INT. JOOK JOINT — NIGHT

An air of simmering violence, with dancing, drinking and gambling in the hazy, flickering madhouse.

Charley Patton, neck wrapped in a filthy, blood-soaked rag, sings "Moon Going Down" hoarsely, strenuously, as a vexed Willie Brown backs him on guitar.

CHARLEY

Aw, that moon gone down, baby / Clarksdale sun 'bout to shine / Rosetta Henry tol' me—

WILLIE

Man, I don' want you hangin' 'round!

CHARLEY

Oh, where were you now, baby? / Clarksdale Mill burned down!

BULLET WILLIAMS, thoroughly soused, wails away on harmonica with middle-aged ROSETTA HENRY hanging onto him. A ruffian named HORSE eyes Rosetta lustily.

CHARLEY

There's a house o'er yonder, painted all over green. (spoken) Boy, you know I know it's over there—

WILLIE

Some o' the finest young womens, Lord, a man most ever seen—

Rosetta and harp-playing Bullet stumble into Charley, who throws them onto Willie, who angrily throws them against a wall. Charley gasps, clutches his throat and keeps singing.

CHARLEY

I was evil at midnight when I heard that local blow. (spoken) Boy, I's gettin' lonesome—

WILLIE (ANGRY)

Same here, buddy—

Jostled by annoyed dancers, then elbowing Horse, Bullet is pushed down into a chair and doused with hootch. Horse glares at him murderously, moving in, as alarmed Rosetta retreats.

Frustrated Willie tries to sing as Charley blocks him from the dancers, poking Willie, clowning with his guitar.

> WILLIE
>
> *Oh, the smokestack's black an' the bell it shine like gold—*

> CHARLEY
>
> You shuckin', boy! You knows it look good to me!

> WILLIE
>
> You on yo' own, ol' clown you—

Willie bolts as Charley sings. He passes Horse, who aims a pistol at stupefied Bullet and shoots. Charley hits the deck. The dancing ensues.

Blues harp in hand, Bullet calmly stares up at Horse.

> ROSETTA
>
> Bullet! You dead!

> BULLET
>
> Naw, I ain't dead.

> HORSE (BLOWING ON GUN)
>
> Huh.

Bullet rises and strolls into the kitchen as Charley, flat on his back, resumes singing.

CHARLEY

Gonna move to Alabama, gonna move to Alabama /
Graveyard to be yo' home—

79. EXT. GRAVEL ROAD — NIGHT

Charley can be heard singing as Robert walks through the pitch stillness wearing a hat, dark suit and white shirt, guitar slung onto his back. He carries his whiskey bottle.

Seething Willie, walking in the opposite direction, bottle in hand as well, passes Robert without recognizing him.

ROBERT

Say, Willie Brown.

WILLIE

Now, who the hell—God damn: Little Robert. Let me take a look at you. Where you been? It's well nigh—

ROBERT

Coupla years now. Been all over, man. Playin' an' makin' my move, y'know. Gettin' my licks.

WILLIE (DRINKING)

Look like you been to the moon. Hmmm—what's that on yo' eye?

An odd white dot covers part of Robert's left eye.

ROBERT

Aw, nothin' much. Been gettin' it from time to time.

WILLIE

One o' them eclipses.

> ROBERT (DRINKING)

Yeah. All them womens, likely.

> WILLIE

See you got yo' gui-tar. Y'know ol' Charley's playin' over yonder jook, singin' like a dog. Bertha Lee's chopped his throat up good.

> ROBERT

I heard she singin' with 'im still.

> WILLIE

Oh, they in love, but he's alone tonight. He's ready for you. You go cut that motherfucker now.

Each pats the other's shoulder as they part.

80. INT. JOOK JOINT — NIGHT

Straining hard in the flickering dimness, Charley sings amid the dancers, sucking on a whiskey bottle.

> CHARLEY

I got me a stone pony, don't ride Shetlands no more /
You can find my stone pony hooked t'my rider's door—

To the side, Bullet drinks hootch with a grotesque crimson splotch on his chest.

> ROSETTA

Bullet, you here drinkin' still? Don't you know you been shot?

> BULLET

Naw, I ain't shot.

ROSETTA

Oh, yes, you is, Bull. I'm gonna get yo' hat, so you can get out 'fore ol' Horse come back an' kill you sure enough.

BULLET

All right. You want me to go.

Rosetta puts the cap on his head. Bottle in hand, Bullet exits into the yard and drops dead. Robert turns from the hootch stand, steps over Bullet and enters the jook.

CHARLEY

Got me a stone pony, don't ride Shetlands no more /
You can find my stone pony hooked to my rider's door—

Robert pushes through and starts playing his guitar behind Charley, who glances back at him. When Charley finishes a verse, Robert challenges him by trading random verses.

CHARLEY

Well, I didn't come here to steal nobody's brown / Jus'
stopped by here to keep you from stealin' mine!

ROBERT

Hello, Central, what's the matter with yo' line? / Come
a storm last night an' tore the wire down!

VOICES

Go stranger! Get 'im Charley! Play it!

A great duel is being waged. Charley, Robert's elder by twenty years, fights hard. Intense Robert is brilliantly rousing. A dizzying rhythm.

CHARLEY

Ain't got no job, mama, rollin' through this world /
When I leave now, mama, goin' further down the road—

The crowd urges Charley on with coins and booze. Robert tosses
his hat away, and Charley tries to block him from the dancers.
Robert turns to the wall, smiling.

ROBERT

Said when I leave here mama goin' further down the
road / If I get back here won't never be bad no mo'—

Robert turns around to see Charley clutch his throat and gag.
But the older man improvises yet another verse.

CHARLEY

An' my baby got a heart like a piece of railroad steel /
An' . . . an'—

Charley gasps. Clowning no more, he struggles to go on.

ROBERT

Sit down, Charley—

CHARLEY

My baby got . . . she got—

ROBERT

Got you, Charley. Time to sit down.

CHARLEY

—got a heart of railroad steel / An' if I leave here this
mornin' don' say, "Daddy how you feel?"

Charley chokes and bolts out the jook. Robert shouts on in the maelstrom, alone.

DISSOLVE TO

The jook is at its most feverish pitch. As Robert sings his seductive dance number, "Walking Blues," a jet-black youth named JOHNNY SHINES studies his scintillating guitar work.

ROBERT

Woke up this mornin', feelin' 'round fo' my shoes / Oo-now, got these ol' walkin' blues—

Robert sees young Johnny, 20, copping his licks and turns away.

ROBERT

Lord, I feel like blowin' my ol' lonesome home. / Got up this mornin' see my Calletta gone—

A woman dances for Robert as another puts money into his guitar. Oblivious, Robert eyes Johnny as he studies his hands; while the dancing continues he slips out the jook.

81. EXT. CORNFIELD — MIDNIGHT

Walking with guitar, Robert hears coughing and gagging amid the stalks. He sees Charley stagger out, clutching his bloody bandaged throat. Spotting Robert, Charley feigns bravado.

CHARLEY

I'll kill 'em all, those charlies. I'll git 'em, I'll bust 'em up—

ROBERT

Who you foolin', man—

CHARLEY

Jus' lookin' to whup some pink ass. So happy I could shout an' shit—

He starts gagging and choking frightfully.

ROBERT

I'm headin' 'cross this field to that jook over yonder. C'mon man, le's go—

CHARLEY

Cain't. Goin' back to Holly Ridge so Bertha Lee won't flay me none. I git you next time.

Robert turns to go, pausing when Charley gags again. He gasps for air, facing solemn Robert. A grotesque pathos.

ROBERT

You the best ever was, Charley Patton. Best ever was.

Coughing, gagging, Charley stands on buckling knees, watching Robert head for the faraway jook. Behind Charley patrons from the first jook search for their musicians.

VOICES

Stranger, play! Charley! Where ol' Charley? Charley! Come back—

Charley trudges back.

DISSOLVE TO

82. **INT. ROADSIDE JOOK — WEE HOURS**

Robert sits in another crammed den, singing "Sweet Home Chicago." A woman dances for him holding her skirt hem high.

> ROBERT
>
> *Ohhhh, baby, don't you want to go? / Back to the land o' California, to my sweet home, Chicago?*

She shakes her ass in Robert's face. Her seething boyfriend sees Robert kiss it tenderly.

DISSOLVE TO

83. **EXT. FRIARS POINT LOT — LATE AFTERNOON**

The enormous crowd carouses in an empty grass lot as Robert shouts "Sweet Home Chicago" over a driving rhythm.

> ROBERT
>
> *Now one an' one is two, an' two an' two is four / I'm heavy loaded baby, I'm booked, I got to go—*

White policemen set up roadblocks as the mob grows. Two rednecks stomp to the beat on a rooftop, dumping their beer on the black revelers below.

84. **EXT. GRAVEL ROAD — MORNING**

Marching along beside the field, natty Robert hears the rumble of a crop duster and looks up. While he swigs his bottle, Goat passes on his rickety bike and swipes it.

The unseen plane swoops down with jarring suddenness, sending Goat into a ditch as hundreds of advertising flyers flutter down from the sky. Robert laughs and treks on, grabbing a flyer out of the air and reading it.

FLYER

THE DEATH OF CHARLEY PATTON! Poor ol' Charley's had one big "Spoonful" too many, so he's gone "Down the Dirt Road" where the "High Sheriff" can't find him. Buy Charley's last great hit "Poor Me" at POWELL'S MUSIC in Jackson TODAY!"

Staring at the page with dismay, Robert's pace accelerates.

85. EXT. LULA — AFTERNOON

The tiny town is thronged by black people mourning the death of Charley Patton. Loud African drumming resounds.

In a lot by the railroad tracks, two youths, a hooting fifer and pounding bass drummer named OTHAR and SID, dance atop a mule cart playing "The Devil's Dream." The mourners bump and grind to the frenzied, mesmerizing West African rhythm.

Atop the cart, propped upright in an open casket behind the performers, the body of Charley Patton looks on.

Robert stands on the crowd's edge watching the amazing scene. He sees REVEREND SIN-KILLER GRIFFIN climb on the cart with a bullhorn and, waving his arms, command the crowd's attention as Sid and Othar reluctantly give way and hop down.

SIN-KILLER

Brothers an' sisters, our subject in this lamentable hour is "There's Nothin' to Do in Hell"!

> VOICES

All right! That's it! C'mon now!

> SIN-KILLER

You know, it look to me like you're ol' preacher Sin-Killer here sees lotsa folks jus' wanna go to Hell!

> VOICES

Yessuh! That's right! Tell it!

Robert guzzles whiskey, passing his bottle to Othar and Sid. They huddle in conspiracy as the preacher continues.

> SIN-KILLER

Asked why, the sin seller said there's too much to do in Heaven! Every mornin' you got to put out the moon an' the stars an' then hang out the sun!

Grinning a bit, dead Charley stands behind the preacher as Othar and Sid help Robert onto the cart, as if he's blind.

> SIN-KILLER

Said he'd jus' rather go to Hell an' do nothin' but keep his feets to the fire! Good God, y'all!

> VOICES

Aaaamennnnn. We gonna see Himmmmm—

Sid and Othar briefly confer with Sin-Killer, who approaches "blind" Robert, sitting on a simple chair with his guitar.

> SIN-KILLER

Bless you, my son. You too shall be heard.

He turns to the crowd.

SIN-KILLER

My brothers an' my sisters, we have our brother Blind
Boy Bob here to bring us all closer to God! Sing it
now!

As "Blind Boy Bob" starts playing the opening chords to "If I
Had Possession over Judgement Day," Sin-Killer steps beside an
OLD DRUNK.

OLD DRUNK

You line ninety-nine whores up against the wall, I bet
you a nickel I fuck 'em all—

Behind Sin-Killer, Robert suddenly stands, foot stomping, blind
no more. The roused crowd picks up his beat as he shouts out
his audacious song into the tumult.

ROBERT

*If I had possession, over Judgement Day / The womens
I'm lovin' wouldn't have no right to PRAY!*

Sin-Killer rushes back over and grabs his bullhorn as Robert
faces dead Charley, performing for him with abandon.

ROBERT

*I rolled an' I tumbled an' I cried the whole night long /
Woke up this mornin', my best friend Charley—GONE!*

On cue, the bass drum explodes as Sid and Othar incite the mob
into a massive tribal dance-chant.

FIFER & DRUMMER

*Charley Patton dead an' gone, left us here to weep an'
moan / Ohhhhh—*

Feet stomping to the irresistible beat, fighting for his audience, Sin-Killer raves through his bullhorn, his words lost in the uproar.

SIN-KILLER

I say to you, I say to you when He come down His hair, chilluns, His hair gonna be like lamb's wool! An' His eyes—His eyes like flames o' fire! Great balls o' fire, y'all, flamin' from His head! An' he ain't dead! 'Cause everyone know He the Son of the true livin' God!

MASS CHANT

Charley Patton dead an' gone, left us here to weep an' moan / Ohhhhhhhh—

From the edge of the riotous scene we see Robert facing the upright casket, dancing, chanting, playing guitar, as the maniacal preacher dances, bounding, shouting vainly.

MASS CHANT

Charley Patton dead an' gone, left us here to weep an' moan / Ohhhhhhhh—

SIN-KILLER

An' he gonna have a tree before the twelve manners of food! Food to feed this ol' world, y'all! An' the leaves—the leaves to be healin' damnation! An' that big ol' racial rock that you can set behind, the wind can't blow at you no more—

Two WHITE COPS eye the assembly. Robert and Sin-Killer dance atop the mule cart with others now. People beat anything vibrant: oil drums, chairs, tree trunks. The flood of rhythm overflows. A crop duster is heard swooping low.

MASS CHANT

Charley Patton dead an' gone, left us here to weep an'
moan / Ohhhhhhhh—

A curtain of fluttering flyers descends with the night. Bedlam.
The body of Charley Patton looks on.

86. EXT. GRAVEL ROAD — NIGHT

Robert whistles while walking. A police car overtakes him. The
two cops hop out and drag Robert behind some bushes.

Beaten, Robert slumps to the ground. One lawman bends over
him as the second examines his guitar.

COP I

Yeah, it's him. He's got the bad eye.

COP 2

Mmm, a Gibson.

As he sets to smash the guitar, weak Robert gropes for it.

SIN-KILLER

Wait fellas! Hold on! Mercy now!

The preacher rushes forth from the police car. Sin-Killer stands
over Robert, who lies in a mess of fallen flyers.

SIN-KILLER

The moral's yours, son, 'cause it's mine. You best
believe it if y'know what's good.

He exits. The cop drops the guitar and follows him. Bloodied
Robert sits up, holding his stomach.

87. EXT. CALLETTA'S SHACK — NIGHT

Robert trudges over to Calletta's candlelit window. Standing
naked before a mirror in the pink candlelit room, Calletta mas-
sages her magnificent body with a thick oil.

88. INT. CALLETTA'S BEDROOM — NIGHT

Enraptured Calletta continues her sensuous massage.

> ROBERT (O.S.)
> Calletta? You still want me?

Startled, she turns to see him enter.

> CALLETTA
> Oh, my God, oh, Robert—

Tearfully she embraces him, burying his face in her breasts as
they descend to the bed.

DISSOLVE TO

Darkness. Silence. Their bodies shift in the bed.

> ROBERT (HUSHED)
> It's on me, Calletta. Me. All fear. Been nervous 'bout
> what's goin' on. Calletta?

> CALLETTA (SLEEPY)
> Mmmmmmmmmmm—

> ROBERT (HUSHED)
> Like I'm between two dangers, where I sleep an' where
> I start. Got me a life that I don't really understand
> myself. Me an' my friends we fool around, they can't
> help me an' I can't help them.

> CALLETTA (SLEEPY)
>
> Robert, marry me.

A momentary lull.

> ROBERT (HUSHED)
>
> It's like this dream comin' back to me: I was a li'l boy walkin', jus' walkin', lookin' for his father—

DISSOLVE TO

89. INT. COURTHOUSE — AFTERNOON

A plain office with pale green cinderblock walls. Robert, head shaved, slowly signs their marriage certificate.

As Calletta signs he dons his hat and abruptly exits. She smiles awkwardly at the white Justice of the Peace.

90. EXT. COURTHOUSE STEPS — AFTERNOON

Calletta joins Robert as they descend the steps.

> ROBERT
>
> Now we gonna keep this secret, hear? We can have yo' party, the way you want, but it's gonna be a secret—

91. EXT. CALLETTA'S SHACK — AFTERNOON

Two groups of three girls and boys bounce gleefully, clapping to a rhythm. Esau pauses to watch, book in hand.

Calletta stands at a kettle of water boiling over a fire, doing a wash. With a long staff she stirs the clothes.

GIRLS

*Steal up, you boys, don't slight us none / 'Cause them
you slight won't have no fun!*

BOYS

Hey satisfied! Hey satisfied!

Still rubbing his eye, Esau walks over to his mother. He points
to a caterpillar crawling up her wooden staff.

ESAU

Mama! Look!

CALLETTA

A baby caterpillar, Esau!

Esau nudges it onto his open book. The long wormlike insect
larva crawls over the printed page.

ESAU

Does he know anything?

CALLETTA

He knows some simple tasks an' things.

ESAU

He still gonna know it when he's a butterfly?

CALLETTA

No, Esau—once he gets his wings he'll forget.

ESAU

When I get my wings will I forget?

CALLETTA

Not if you an angel. Angels don't never forget.

The boys and girls jump up and down in a circle around a cute little girl in the middle.

BOYS

See that girl with the red dress on? / She gonna buck-dance all night long!

GIRLS

Hey satisfied! Hey satisfied!

Robert exits the shack with his guitar. As Calletta jabs her staff at the water he kisses her and moves on.

CALLETTA

Say, Hot Stuff! When you gettin' ready?

ROBERT

Already am. Jus' takin' a little walk. Now remember:
it's a secret—

CALLETTA

Dinner's at eight! I'll look good enough to eat!

ROBERT

You best be waitin' on me!

She dips the staff into the water as he heads for the levee and raises a pair of Robert's striped trousers.

CHILDREN

Hey satisfied! Hey satisfied!

92. EXT. LEVEE — TWILIGHT

The skies are ablaze with the setting sun as Robert marches atop the dark green flood wall.

93. EXT. RIVERSIDE — NIGHT

Robert passes some cows chewing grass by the river. He sits and huddles over his guitar, softly humming and picking "Come On in My Kitchen."

A young cowherd—Johnny Shines, seen earlier at the jook—sits unnoticed in a grounded rowboat with a whiskey bottle and dormant guitar as bald Robert doffs his hat to sing and strum chords to himself.

> ROBERT (LOW)
>
> *Oh, oh, she gone, I know she won't come back / I taken her last nickel out her nation sack. / You better come on, hmmm hmmmm hmm hmm / It's gonna be rainin' outdoors—*

Johnny turns and stands as Robert utters a spoken passage, his guitar trembling in the nervous air.

> ROBERT (LOW)
>
> *Baby, can't you hear the wind howl? Oh, how the wind do howl—*

Robert spots Johnny, clutches his guitar and heads up the riverside. Johnny calls "Hey!" and catches up with him.

> ROBERT
>
> You coppin', man—I don't like it. You wanna cut me then c'mon, le's go.

Disdainfully he brushes past Johnny heading on toward the moaning cows. Johnny catches up again. They stop to talk.

> JOHNNY
>
> I ain't tryin' to cut you. I can't do that, I seen you play—you the man o' the day. What you doin' here 'round Lula, Friars Point, anyway? I'm John Shines; you call me Johnny—

He takes a hit of liquor and passes the bottle to Robert.

> ROBERT
>
> What I'm doin' here? What you think I'm doin' here?

> JOHNNY
>
> Money? It's all over in Arkansas. West Helena, man, over yonder—

Drinking, the two youths stare across the Mississippi River. Cows moan in the gusty darkness behind them.

> JOHNNY
>
> So, man—I'll take you there. You goin' with me? Huh? You goin'?

Robert ponders the dark whispering river.

94. INT. CALLETTA'S SHACK — NIGHT

In her tight red party dress, Calletta rushes about setting food and drinks on the candlelit table and choosing a record for the Victrola.

Hearing footsteps outside, expectantly she opens the door. But no one is there.

95. **EXT. BOAT ON RIVER — NIGHT**

His back to the skiff's bow, Johnny rows away from shore, talking low. Robert sits opposite to him, drinking.

> JOHNNY
>
> West Helena's got the best musicianers anywhere, man. Sonny Boy Williamson's there, Peetie Wheatstraw, too, a big kid named Chester, calls hisself "Howlin' Wolf"—these ain't some drunken niggers jookin' in a field, man. You find record jobbers lookin' in. Go there, join a record company; hell, make some o' that money—

Robert drinks up. The cows moan behind as the little skiff moves through the silken black water. A handsome wild duck paddles over, following alongside.

Johnny keeps rowing, the bottle goes back and forth. A small flatboat looms distantly.

> ROBERT
>
> What's comin'?

> JOHNNY
>
> Can't tell—

The vessel drifts closer. Laughing female voices emerge. Obscure figures grouped on deck become discernible.

> ROBERT (HUSHED)
>
> Womens—

Johnny rows hard to intersect the flatboat's path, the duck quacking behind. Thirty yards ahead, the craft floats slowly by. Johnny quits rowing. Robert stares.

JOHNNY (HUSHED)

The *Katy Adams*—

Standing on board, six painted black wenches chatter, laugh, search the shore. As the skiff drifts closer they pass by, pointing merrily. They lift their skirts and jiggle the sack of coins each has hanging between her thighs.

JOHNNY (HUSHED)

It's them Memphis whores, man, goin' down to Rosedale—

A black man with a gun steers at the stern. Apart from the six, ethereal Virginia moves helplessly along the back edge.

WHORES

Ooooo! Hey! Pretty boy! Want it!

Robert holds his hat as the boat blends with the blackness. Virginia disappears last. The duck quacks once.

96. EXT. ARKANSAS SHORE — NIGHT

Water slaps against the skiff as it drifts in. Johnny hops off and pulls it ashore; Robert steps off the boat holding two guitars. Silently the duck looks on.

ROBERT

Let's move—

JOHNNY

We'll get my cousin Calvin to drive us there.

Johnny overturns the boat, throws a fishing net on it, covers it with leaves and weed, then exits with Robert.

DISSOLVE TO

97. EXT. RISING SUN CAFE — NIGHT

Hand-painted letters on the cracked pane read "RiSiNG SuN CaFE." And below: "moRe then Just a BaR" and "tamales." While a jug band inside wreaks gay delirium, a vendor pushes his cart up the street.

> SHRIMP VENDOR
> Dead shrimmmmp, shrimp man out here—

He pushes the cart past well-dressed black men and women who mill about in the street, talking and drinking.

A signboard leans against the door announcing "TAMPA RED'S HOKUM BAND!"

98. INT. RISING SUN CAFE — NIGHT

Dangling bulbs with cardboard reflectors swing and flicker in the loud joint. Strutting on the bandstand is the diminutive singer and female impersonator FRANKIE JAXON, costumed like a hotel bellhop, now mocking a bug-eyed sideman blowing on a big glass jug to "My Daddy Rocks Me."

> FRANKIE
> *My man rocks me with one steady roll / It makes no difference if he's hot or cold—*

In baggy suit, red beret and string tie, dumpy TAMPA RED slides his steel guitar, kazoo tooting, leading his band. Handsome GEORGIA TOM, so very cool in fur coat and fedora cocked over an eye, takes a brandy snifter to his piano.

> FRANKIE

If you can't sell it, sit on it!

Tom takes his cue and pounds the keys with authority.

> FRANKIE

Looked at the clock, the clock struck one / I said, "Aw, Honey, let's have some fun." / He started rockin' me with one big steady roll—

99. **INT. JALOPY — NIGHT**

Young CALVIN FRAZIER drives with Johnny beside him. Robert is in the back seat drinking, picking his guitar.

> JOHNNY

You need an agent, man. I be yo' agent.

> CALVIN

Hacksaw, he put them guys in the shade. He got an agent.

> ROBERT

I don't need no damn agent. That white guy you talkin' 'bout, he jus' be standin' there.

> CALVIN

Say man, what name you gonna be?

100. **EXT. JALOPY ON RIVER ROAD — NIGHT**

Calvin drives the sputtering jalopy along the immense river.

> JOHNNY (O.S.)

How 'bout "Sudan Washington"?

> CALVIN (O.S.)

No, no—he's "Terrible Slug."

IOI. INT. RISING SUN CAFE — NIGHT

Frankie vamps his way into "She Loves So Good."

> FRANKIE

> *I got a gal, she's low an' squatty / I mean, boys, she'll suit anybody. / She loves so good—*

Frankie serenades the jug blower on hands and knees before crawling over to Tampa Red.

> FRANKIE

> *An' everybody wants her 'cause she loves so . . . peculiar—*

IO2. EXT. RISING SUN CAFE — NIGHT

Calvin parks the jalopy outside the roadhouse. The three youths enter, Robert toting his guitar.

IO3. INT. RISING SUN CAFE — NIGHT

On hands and knees, pretending to stroke dumpy Tampa Red's groin, Frankie mocks a popular blues.

> FRANKIE

> *How long . . . how long . . . how long, Daddy, how long—*

Wearing a wrinkled shirt with rolled sleeves, 47-year-old white talent scout ERNIE OERTLE sips a beer in his chair.

Robert, with a pint of gin at the bar, spots the somewhat dissolute Oertle through the dancers and eyes him fixedly.

FRANKIE

Oh, Mister Tampa, you must be a Florida man!

Standing over Oertle now in tattered suit and hat, unkempt BUDDY BOY HAWKINS pleads with the talent scout, who shakes his head and through bloodshot eyes watches Frankie shine.

FRANKIE

Oooo! How long . . . how long . . . / Oh, jump me now, Papa! Tell me how long—

After annoyed Oertle sends Buddy Boy away, Johnny moves through the crowd and urgently chats with him, pointing at entranced Robert, who studies Tampa Red's guitar playing.

OERTLE (O.S.)

You Robert Johnson?

When Robert turns, he is startled to find himself facing the unshaven white talent scout, Oertle. Beyond them, Frankie is now cradled in pianist Georgia Tom's lap.

GEORGIA TOM

Woman, you readin' that *Ladies Home Journal?*

FRANKIE

Yes, sweet daddy, but I want that *Saturday Evenin' POST!*

DISSOLVE TO

104. INT. RISING SUN CAFE — LATE NIGHT

A driving rhythm rocks the stomping joint. On the bandstand Robert leads Johnny and Calvin on guitar into "I Believe I'll Dust My Broom."

> ROBERT
>
> *I'm gonna get up in the mornin', I believe I'll dust my broom / But now when that black man you done lovin', girl, his friends can get my room—*

Robert's guitar is an alchemy of barrelhouse piano and surging bass rhythms. Dead serious, shaved head shining with sweat, he lowers his shoulder and rocks toward the dancers.

> ROBERT
>
> *I'm gonna write a letter, telephone every town I know / If I can't find her in West Helena, she be in East Monroe, I know—*

Buddy Boy resumes his plea to Oertle, who instead watches Robert as joyous Frankie bumps and grinds across the floor.

> FRANKIE
>
> Oh, honey! Oh, kiss me now! Right there!

DISSOLVE TO

105. INT. RISING SUN CAFE — MIDNIGHT

An exciting epiphany of song and dance. "Dust My Broom" thunders with Georgia Tom on piano, Frankie Jaxon hooting and strutting, bald Robert Johnson singing and wringing his guitar, with four seated guitarists, knees interlocked and guitars kissing, creating a wall of rhythm from behind.

Singing, rocking, playing guitar with all his might, Robert is in control out front on the bandstand.

> ROBERT

> *I'm goin' call up Chiney, see is my good girl over there /*
> *If I can't find her on Philippines Island, she must be in*
> *Ethiopia somewhere—*

Soused Oertle beholds Robert's brilliance in the chaos. Robert dips and pivots on the platform. A frenzied peak.

> FRANKIE

> Oh, if I die, let me die while I'm happy! I'm dyin' for you, Lord! Hot damn!

106. EXT. RISING SUN CAFE — AFTER MIDNIGHT

Hunched over, Oertle ushers Robert away from the exhausted, milling crowd. When Buddy Boy sees them pause in the shadows, he turns and sadly heads into the night.

> OERTLE

> I got your name from Henry Speir down in Jackson. My name's Ernie Oertle, field rep for the American Record Company. An', y'know, I like your style; you're doin' somethin' strange an' good. How many o' them songs you got, all told?

> ROBERT

> Twenty, thirty. But they jus' air songs. As many as there is, I got.

> OERTLE

Long as you got two. An' they can't be the same. Now
come with me—

Once they move farther away, furtive Oertle flashes some cash.

> OERTLE (LOW)

That's twenty bucks there, waitin' for you. Cold cash.
Now you got to remember this goddamn deal's dead
serious, son, meanin' you're a professional from here
on in, a recordin' artist with the American Record
Company. They're as tight as two fingers in a one-
finger fanny; everything's on time and in order, in
that way. So ten in the mornin'. I'll meet you here
with the dough; we'll grab a coupla beers and get
you on that train. You with me?

> ROBERT (LOW)

Yes, sir.

> OERTLE (LOW)

Okay. Then tomorrow I'll tell you about San Antonio,
Texas, an' how you'll go find the Gunter Hotel, an' a
fella there named Law—

107. EXT. FIELDS — WEE HOURS

Calletta clutches her shawl, rushing into the far fields.

108. EXT. BATH HOUSE — WEE HOURS

Robert, Calvin and Johnny approach a sign over a storefront
reading "West Helena / BATHS / Colored."

> CALVIN
>
> Hacksaw, he said they put his head in some kind o' horn, an' he have to pull his head out for the words, then put it back in to sing. But he said they keep you good an' drunk, all likkered up, for free.

They pause beneath the sign.

> JOHNNY
>
> This is it, man. Room's upstairs—

> CALVIN
>
> We catch you 'fore too long

109. **EXT. LEVEE — WEE HOURS**

Calletta hurries along atop the flood wall. Finally she stops where, weeping, she holds herself sorrowfully.

110. **INT. BATH HOUSE — WEE HOURS**

A barren, impersonal room. Robert removes his shirt, drapes it over his upright guitar and slips into bed.

The sad low chant of a BLACKBERRY VENDOR drifts up from the street. An eerie, faraway calling.

> VENDOR (O.S.)
>
> *Blackberry black . . . looka blackberry dozen an' blackberry fine . . . ease yo' black blood ol' friend o' mine—*

Facing the open window, lying on his side, Robert stares distantly, biting his lip. He rolls over and ponders the darkness.

> VENDOR (O.S.)

Yessuh, how much—

DISSOLVE TO

III. EXT. SAN ANTONIO TRAIN DEPOT — DAWN

A cold mist at daybreak. Standing outside the depot, a tall, stout black man wearing three gray overcoats and no shoes is playing guitar and singing joyfully, his big voice ringing.

> RAGTIME

Heyyy, Jonah, haaalll-lelujah! Heyyy, Jonah, preachin'
in that wilderness—

The charismatic hobo smiles while playing to the camera. He strums his old guitar vigorously.

> RAGTIME

Go down yonder to the bottom of the ship, / See you
can find the dirty blue-eyed Christian / "Soon to come
after," so say the Lord. / Could not find that blue-eyed
Christian—

With ancient bamboo panpipes hanging from his neck, he merrily stomps his bare foot, his breath visible in the chill.

> RAGTIME

Had Brother Jonah sent overboard, / Cast the bird an'
dropped the seed, / Dropped the seed 'long came the root,
/ From the root is that strong vine—

A strolling COP with a billy club pauses.

RAGTIME

*From the vine is that strong shade, / Under that shade
Brother Jonah laid—*

COP

Let's move along now, Ragtime.

Smiling at the passing officer, strumming loudly, barefoot Ragtime doesn't miss a beat. A closer look tells us that his guitar has no strings.

RAGTIME

*When I get to heaven, I will sit an' tell, / I escaped both
Death an' Hell. / Heyyy, Jonah, haall-lelujah! Preachin'
in that wilderness!*

Strings ringing stringlessly, singing gaily, Ragtime wanders off as a Texas & Pacific freight and passenger train arrives.

SUPER: San Antonio, Texas, November 1936

112. EXT. TRAIN DEPOT PLATFORM — EARLY MORNING

A TRAIN CALLER chants as passengers embark and disembark.

TRAIN CALLER

All out for the Sunshine Special! Change cars on the
T.P.! Fort Worth! Dallas! Mineola! Garden City! El
Dorado! Tex-ark-ana!

Wearing a dark suit and white shirt, weary Robert traverses the platform with his guitar slung onto his back.

> TRAIN CALLER
>
> Change from the Katy! Pine Bluff! Magnolia! Hopeville! Territory!

> TAMALE VENDOR
>
> Got red-hot tamales! Got yo' red-hot tamales! Oh, tamales, oh! Oh, tamales, ah! Got red-hot tamales!

Robert buys a tamale and eats it en route to the street.

113. EXT. HAT SHOP — DAY

Fixing the brim on his new brown fedora, Robert exits the shop and walks out into the brilliant sunlight.

114. EXT. SAN ANTONIO STREET — AFTERNOON

Robert wanders along eating another tamale, tossing it into a bin and moving on. A tramp fishes for the refuse, then tastes the wrapper.

115. EXT. GUNTER HOTEL — SUNSET

Pausing outside a dingy bar, Robert beholds the impressive fa-cade of the Gunter Hotel across the street. A deafening, shrill police siren scares him, and he ducks into the bar.

116. INT. BAR — SUNSET

In the noisy joint Robert is at the bar, finishing a pint. He signals for another round. As he scans the reeling room, he's joined by husky WILLIE MAE CROSS, 42.

> WILLIE MAE
>
> I's a handsome woman. An' you's a handsome man.

ROBERT (TO BARTENDER)

Make that two, nigger.

WILLIE MAE

I's Willie Mae Cross.

ROBERT

Bob Johnson.

A man kneeling on the floor blows a blues harp as loud as can be, straining mightily for the impossible note. Kneeling next to him, a delirious drunk pleads for the harp player to stop.

WILLIE MAE

You got money, lover?

DISSOLVE TO

117. INT. GUNTER HOTEL LOBBY — TWILIGHT

A well-appointed lobby with white clientele and hotel staff personnel passing to and fro in the pale, dreamy light. From a radio, Miss Ivey Anderson with the Duke Ellington Orchestra sings "Stormy Weather."

Beneath cardboard letters spelling "Happy Thanksgiving," a lithe young blonde named FAYE, with hotel vest undone, scans the lobby, her finger tapping a hissing radiator.

RADIO

Don't know why there's no sun up in the sky, stormy weather—

Robert enters and pauses awkwardly. Lovely Faye catches his eye, rubbing her ass against the warm radiator coils.

A BELLHOP in a snappy red outfit queries Robert. As he does, Faye interjects, slipping the bellhop some change.

> BELLHOP
>
> The studio's on the seventh floor, but I'm afraid the folks up there—

> FAYE
>
> I've got him, Ronnie Wayne. Now c'mon, boy, this away—

She leads him toward an Exit sign.

118. INT. HOTEL ROOM — TWILIGHT

Faye takes Robert into the small, cluttered room. Shapely C. J. DARWIN shuts the door as Faye undresses by a table.

> C.J.
>
> Hold your peace, good boy.

Robert turns to see Faye drop her skirt, then turns back.

> ROBERT
>
> I'm lookin' for Mr. Law.

> C.J.
>
> I'm Mrs. C. J. Darwin. An' this child here's my baby sister Faye.

On the bed, naked Faye eyes Robert on all fours, purring.

> C.J.
>
> We thought we'd have you perform a coupla numbers for us, Mistuh Recordin' Star—

As C.J. shuts her eyes, purses her lips, loosens a button, Robert twists the knob and opens the door a slit.

119. INT. HOTEL HALLWAY — LATER

Discreetly Robert shuts the door and steals down the hall, ducking into an Exit door as a businessman rounds the far corner and strolls pensively to his room.

120. INT. RECORDING STUDIO — NIGHTFALL

A darkened, vacant chamber. Light sprays through a window onto a wood chair by a stand-up microphone. The studio is a regular hotel room with a makeshift observation window.

Robert enters. He approaches the microphone, then sits, the guitar across his lap. A stillness. Softly, pining sweetly, he sings "Kindhearted Woman" to himself, a capella.

> ROBERT
>
> *I got a kindhearted woman, do anything this world for me. / Got a kindhearted mama, mmm mmm mmm—*

Robert leans forward, his lips near the dead microphone.

> ROBERT
>
> *But these evil-hearted women, man, they will not let me be—*

He looks over his right shoulder, pausing. He rises and delicately leans his guitar against the chair.

> ROBERT
>
> *She's a kindhearted mama, studies evil all the time—*

At the window he examines the curtains.

> ROBERT

You wish to kill me, else to have it on your—

The dim yellow lights switch on. Robert freezes. The calm voice of an Oxfordian Englishman emerges.

> LAW

Easy spider—easy now—

DON LAW is a tall, handsome gentleman in his early thirties, wearing a white shirt with rolled sleeves and a tie. Robert doesn't move as Law steps in and faces him.

> LAW

Good, that's it—Now, may I ask what it is you're looking for?

> ROBERT

Mr. Don Law. Gotta find 'im. The man in charge what's makin' them records. He's expectin' me.

> LAW

I am Mr. Law. Who are you?

> ROBERT

Bob Johnson. One of the talents, sir.

> LAW

Is that guitar yours?

> ROBERT

Yes, sir. She's mine.

> LAW

How'd you make it up here, Bob?

ROBERT

Give 'em my name, sir.

121. INT. RECORDING SUITE — MORNING

Two white assistants, JIMMY and ART, gaze through the observation window into the empty studio as Law and Robert pass by.

LAW

Yes, Mr. Oertle told me about you. He mentioned a nice tune you have, the one about a broom. You're just a youngster, what—twenty-two, twenty-three?

ROBERT

Yessir, that's right, twenty-four, twenty-five—

122. INT. REHEARSAL ROOM — NOON

Cowboy and Mexican musicians mill about, eating sandwiches and drinking steins of beer. A polka band relaxes with their accordions, glockenspiels, and a bass drum reading "ADOLPH and the BOHEMIANS."

Robert sits in a corner, picking his guitar, mumbling. Over him stands Law, a whiskey bottle on the floor between them.

LAW

So where do you hail from, Bob?

ROBERT

The Delta. Yazoo Delta. Clarksdale, Robinsonville. Mississippi, all in around there. Arkansas, West Helena—

LAW

Have you any family to speak of?

ROBERT

A few brothers, sisters scattered about. Guess my mother's down in Commerce. Never knowed my father. Name's Noah. Mmm. Hard to say.

A sensitive man, Law sees Robert lower his gaze and quietly pick his guitar strings.

LAW

So then, getting down to business, we do run things very much on time around here. And you don't just liquor up and play; first we want to know what you play, how you play it, by which I mean words to the songs as well as what instruments you use, and how long you take to do a song. No song may exceed three minutes. Now you'll only do four—we have lots of people to see today. Tell me: do you rehearse much?

ROBERT

—mistreated, reason why . . . yessir, all the time, myself, no one else—

Robert grabs his bottle and drinks, briefly glancing at Law.

LAW

As we've discussed, we furnish you with all the drink you'll need. And when you must relieve yourself it's downstairs, hotel policy. Now, have you ever been behind a microphone?

ROBERT

—wring my hands . . . no, sir, uh-uh.

LAW

Well, we use a Western Electric condenser mike. Since it's been so terribly hot and humid, if or when something goes wrong we can switch to a carbon mike setup. The main thing about this microphone, Bob, is this: you must never forget it is there.

> ROBERT
>
> —slow the dark, slow the dark come down ... Never forget, no, sir.

123. INT. RECORDING BOOTH — AFTERNOON

From the doorway Law calls back to Robert.

> LAW
>
> Say, Bob—we've noticed you tap your foot a lot.

No response. Law addresses Robert via loudspeaker.

> LAW
>
> You do seem rather jittery over there.

> ROBERT (VIA SPEAKER)
>
> This shakin's what keeps me steady, sir.

Law calls over to Jimmy by the door.

> LAW
>
> Get a pillow for his feet.

124. INT. RECORDING STUDIO — LATE AFTERNOON

The red light blinks over solitary Robert, a pillow beneath his foot. He picks the guitar nervously, mumbling, waiting. He swigs his whiskey bottle. Behind the glass stand Law and his assistants by the recording machine, ready to begin.

> LAW (VIA SPEAKER)
>
> Master number 26-29, take one, Robert Johnson, stand by—

Robert mumbles beneath the blinking red light. Law waits.

> ROBERT
>
> —ooo wee, don't nobody seem to know me, everybody pass me by—

> LAW (VIA SPEAKER)
>
> Silence. Ready now—

Abruptly Robert stands, turns his chair around and sets it down in the corner facing the converging walls. He slides the microphone in front of him and sits back down.

> ROBERT
>
> Yessir, le's go.

> LAW (VIA SPEAKER)
>
> All right then—it's rolling, Bob—

The blue light glows as Robert leans toward the microphone, playing "Crossroads" with a chugging bass rhythm.

> ROBERT
>
> *I went to the crossroads, fell down on my knees, / Asked the Lord above, "Have mercy, save poor Bob if you please—"*

His lips are inches from the microphone.

> ROBERT
>
> *Sun goin' down, sun gonna catch me here / Haven't got no lovin' sweet woman to love an' feel my care—*

Eyes widening, Law studies Robert as Art checks the machines. Robert sings with eyes shut, teeth clenched.

ROBERT

You can run, you can run, tell my friendboy Willie
Brown, / Lord, that I'm standin' at the crossroads, babe,
I believe I'm sinkin' down—

DISSOLVE TO

Blades of light slice the dim studio, the blue bulb blinks, as the
camera semicircles Robert singing "Terraplane Blues."

ROBERT

An' I feel so lonesome, you hear me when I moan / Who's
boon drivin' my Terraplane for you since I been gone?

The studio light is switched on, casting a jaundiced pall.

ROBERT

I said I flashed my lights, mama, your horn won't even
blow. (spoken) Someone foolin' with the battery in
that machine. *I got a short in this connection hoo!*
wherever, way down below—

The camera pans the faces of Jimmy, Art, then Law, who listens
and nods knowingly.

ROBERT

Mr. Highwayman, plea-hease don't block the road /
Mr. Highwayman, plee-hease! don't block the road—

Reaching for emotive peaks, as the camera circles him Robert
throws his head away from the microphone.

ROBERT

—'cause she registerin' a cold one hundred. / I'm booked,
I gotta go—

I25. INT. RECORDING BOOTH — NIGHTFALL

A displeased Law shakes his head, muttering to Art.

> LAW
>
> He keeps turning away from the mike. That damn head of his.

But Law senses something very unusual is going on, and when the last chords cease he turns to Art.

> LAW
>
> There's no point in doing anyone else today. We must get whatever we can before this boy leaves.

I26. INT. REHEARSAL ROOM — TWILIGHT

German, Mexican and Texan cowboy musicians drink, practice and chat while Art draws the window curtains.

> LAW (O.S. VIA SPEAKER)
>
> Master number 26-31, take one, Robert Johnson. Stand by—

> ART
>
> That's it, folks. Mr. Law says you get to go home early.

> ROBERT (O.S. VIA SPEAKER)
>
> *It's the last fair deal gone down / Last fair deal gone down, good Lord, on that Gulfport Island Road—*

The musicians gather their belongings and begin to exit.

> ART
>
> As you leave, please check the schedule posted for tomorrow—

127. INT. RECORDING STUDIO — TWILIGHT

Robert leans into the lively rhythm of "Last Fair Deal Gone Down" as the off-work musicians jam the booth.

> ROBERT
>
> *My Captain's so mean on me / My Captain's so mean,*
> *oh, good Lord, on this Gulfport Island Road—*

Stout ADOLPH HOFNER swigs his beer in the booth, now packed with cowboy, Mexican and polka musicians watching Robert approvingly, excitedly, nodding to the beat.

128. INT. RECORDING BOOTH — NIGHT

With the red bulb blinking over Robert's head, pensive Law studies his ledger sheets, looks out at tired Robert as he stands, then, shaking his head, checks his notes again as if the answer to Robert's brilliance might be found there.

Robert pauses in the doorway with his guitar.

> ROBERT
>
> Night, sir. Hope you got what you need.

> LAW
>
> You know, young man, I don't believe I've yet heard anything quite like those songs of yours. It's hard to imagine where they've come from. Have you any formal schooling?

> ROBERT
>
> In Memphis some, 'til I was ten—'fore they run my stepdad out o' town. But I read an' write okay, an' I can spell.

> LAW

Well, the blues songs I've heard all come from other blues songs, while yours seem closer to—to poetry, to verse, which you must have read in school.

> ROBERT

But see, sir, I don't honor that stuff none. It ain't me.

> LAW

May I ask what is?

> ROBERT

All o' what I been and gonna be. Them songs is my destiny.

Law perceives Robert's formidable intellect.

> ROBERT

Guess I best be on my way, sir.

> LAW

Godspeed, young man. I do hope our roads cross again.

Law stares distantly as Robert's footsteps fade.

129. EXT. TRAIN STATION PLATFORM — AFTER MIDNIGHT

Stillness. Ragtime sleeps on a bench, a dark passenger train behind. Footsteps draw near.

Robert traverses the desolate platform, guitar on his back, toting a suitcase. He boards the car marked "Colored."

Now Robert's somber face appears in the row of blackened windows. A brakeman passes, swinging a lantern.

DISSOLVE TO

130. EXT. CALLETTA'S SHACK — AFTERNOON

An old taxi arrives near the shack, idling as Robert exits it. He proudly holds a wad of cash from his Texas gig, and before paying, he calls for his wife, wanting to show off.

> ROBERT
> Hey, Calletta! Look who's back! Calletta! Esau!
> Come 'ere!

Getting no response, Robert pays the cabbie, who drives off. Now he turns to see some of Calletta's friends leave the shack somberly in dark suits and dresses.

> ROBERT
> Afternoon—Hey there, Alfred—

Confused, Robert stands alone, awkward, shunned by all.

131. INT. CALLETTA'S SHACK — AFTERNOON

Robert puts down his suitcase as little Esau meets him finger-over-lips while a solemn guitar plays behind him.

> ESAU
> Hush—don't wake her yet.

In an open pine wood coffin, Calletta wears her red party dress as Esau's aged GRANDPA, his white-whiskered face aglow with Biblical dignity, softly plays guitar and sings.

GRANDPA

Lord I can't stay here by myself / Can't stay here by myself—

Robert is aghast to see Calletta's crudely gashed wrists.

ESAU

She cut herself.

GRANDPA

I'm gonna weep like a willow, an' moan like a dove / O Lord, I can't stay here by myself, can't stay here by myself—

The distinguished man pauses, his state of shock evident.

GRANDPA

Mmm, that's an old one. Uh-huh. Used to sing her to sleep with it.

Robert is impaled by the moment. Calletta's woeful father studies his stricken visitor.

GRANDPA

Now, we ain't met yet, have we—

Wide-eyed, Robert is mortified.

132. EXT. CALLETTA'S SHACK — AFTERNOON

From the doorway Esau watches dumbstruck Robert leave past oncoming mourners. A couple glares at him trudging off with guitar and suitcase in hand.

FEMALE MOURNER

It's him. Satan hisself.

MALE MOURNER

God damn you, man.

Grievous, Robert hears them but doesn't respond, walking on.

133. EXT. LULA TRAIN DEPOT — LATE AFTERNOON

Robert trudges mechanically into the little depot.

134. INT. LULA TRAIN DEPOT — LATE AFTERNOON

Numb with grief, Robert leans toward the ticket window.

ROBERT

I gotta go.

TICKET AGENT

Where to, boy?

ROBERT

Don't know. It's jus', I gotta go.

Overcome with woe he backs away and sits on a bench, bent
over, holding himself.

ROBERT (CRYING)

I'll go to Hell for you, Calletta. I'll go to Hell for
you—

Over the image emerge the first shimmering, gently descending guitar chords to "Love in Vain."

DISSOLVE TO

135. INT. RECORDING STUDIO — LATE AFTERNOON

Robert plays guitar facing the corner, surrounded by long dark drapes. A blue bulb glows on the wall. Law stands at his microphone as helplessly sad Robert leans forward to sing.

SUPER: Dallas, Texas, June 1937

> ROBERT
>
> *An' I followed her to the station, with a suitcase in my hand / Well it's hard to tell, it's hard to tell, when all your love's in vain / All my love's in vain—*

Robert's lips almost touch the microphone. Law looks on behind the glass. With the studio lights off, the natural half-light intensifies the atmosphere.

> ROBERT
>
> *When the train rolled up to the station, I looked her in the eye / Well, I was lonesome, I felt so lonesome, an' I could not help but cry / All my love's in vain—*

136. INT. RECORDING BOOTH — TWILIGHT

As Law turns his head away, through the window we see Robert singing in his corner, the blue light aglow.

> ROBERT
>
> *When the train, it left the station, with two lights on behind / Well, the blue light was my blues, an' the red light was my mind / All my love's in vain—*

Law dons a pair of bulky headphones, pressing them tightly to his ears as the gentle force of the song swells.

137. INT. REHEARSAL ROOM — TWILIGHT

In the lightless, cluttered little room, the hanging speaker carries the final chords of Robert's desperate plaint. By his vacant chair lie his hat and whiskey bottle.

                    ROBERT (O.S.)
            Ooo-wee-oh woe, all my love's in vain.

138. INT. RECORDING STUDIO — NIGHT

The red bulb blinks. Robert swigs his bottle as the studio light goes on. He lowers the bottle. An ominous air.

Art enters and closes a heavy curtain. He tries moving a bathtub full of water and melting ice as Law looks on, but drags a fan away instead.

Holding his bottle, Robert stares at a skinny black janitor wringing his mop into a bucket. The older man picks up his bucket and, staring back at Robert, slowly exits.

                    LAW (VIA SPEAKER)
        Master number 3-9-8, take one, Robert Johnson.
        Stand by—

The blue bulb aglow, Robert begins with a suspenseful rhythm. Law dons his headset, Art enters the booth.

                    ROBERT
        Early this morning, when you knocked upon my door /
        I said, "Hello Satan, I believe it's time to go"—

Robert's lips almost touch the microphone as he sings "Me and the Devil" clearly, his tone matter-of-fact.

> ROBERT

Me an' the Devil was walkin' side by side / I'm goin' to beat my woman 'til I get satisfied—

139. **INT. RECORDING BOOTH — NIGHT**

Law removes his headphones as the startling song unfolds.

> ROBERT (VIA SPEAKER)

She say she don't see why, that I will dog her 'round. (spoken) Now babe, you ain't doin' me right / *Must be that ol' evil spirit, so deep down in the ground.*

140. **INT. RECORDING STUDIO — NIGHT**

Robert seems to confide in his microphone now.

> ROBERT

You may bury my body down by the highway side / So my ol' evil spirit can get a Greyhound bus, an' ride—

Robert ends the powerful song and drops his head. The red light blinks above him.

DISSOLVE TO

141. **INT. LEVEE CAMP — NIGHT**

SILENT IMAGE: A canopy lit by kerosene lamps. Robert plays to levee workers and women from town. A shirtless tough holds a blade to a woman's throat as they dance.

LAW (VIA SPEAKER)

Well, Bob, I'll have Art here give you your wages for your services, as you're due sixty dollars. That does include your royalty advance.

ROBERT

Yessir, thank you, sir. I be needin' that awhile.

A vicious brawl erupts. The tough is brutally stabbed.

DISSOLVE TO

142. EXT. LEVEE CAMP — NIGHT

SILENT IMAGE: The violence spills outside the tent. Calvin is jumped by a man, whom he fells with a punch. The man shoots Calvin in the wrist; Johnny grabs the gun and shoots the assailant dead as Robert hurries over.

ROBERT (O.S.) (CONT.)

I be needin' that 'cause, see, every man have his share of dignity in this life, sir. Thank you, Mr. Law, sir—

DISSOLVE TO

143. INT. HOUSE PARTY — NIGHT

SILENT IMAGE: Robert, dressed nattily in double-breasted suit, a white flower in his lapel, croons for an all-redneck crowd of dancers. Johnny backs him up with wounded Calvin, who conceals his inability to play.

> LAW (O.S.) (VIA SPEAKER)

Well, Bob, you surely have earned it. You've done particularly well. There is something about you—mark my words, you'll get your dignity yet.

DISSOLVE TO

144. INT. JOOK JOINT — NIGHT

SILENT IMAGE: Hair slicked back, dressed in white, draped by eager women, Robert performs with Johnny and Calvin. He signals Johnny to take the lead, and when Johnny looks back, Robert has vanished. Footsteps on the studio floor.

> ROBERT (O.S.)

Y'know it say in the Bible that man come somewhere east of Eden under God all the same, through love an' pain an' good an' evil consequence like a ship on the sea, to live an' let live—

> LAW (O.S.)

So where will you be heading next, Bob—back home to the Delta?

DISSOLVE TO

145. INT. BOARDINGHOUSE ROOM — NIGHT

SILENT IMAGE: Robert makes love to an aging overweight black woman, who manhandles him onto his back.

> ROBERT (O.S.)

'Cause when you get to the final end you goin' stay anyway, you linger if you like it or not, this life you

don't remember. . . . Yessir, goin' home, you can say
that, sir—

The door opens and the matronly proprietor leads Johnny in,
ending the youth's search for Robert.

DISSOLVE TO

146. EXT. ROADSIDE JOOK — NIGHT

SILENT IMAGE: A sign reads "Bunk's Place" as black men and
women chat and carouse and shoot craps outside.

> LAW (O.S.)
>
> It's always good to go home, Bob. It makes you feel
> so good inside—

DISSOLVE TO

147. EXT. CHARLEY MOLEMAN'S — NIGHT

SILENT IMAGE: A flashing sign reads "CHARLEY MOLEMAN'S"
atop the snow-covered roadhouse. A police car cruises by.

> ROBERT (O.S.)
>
> Now I ain't exactly doin' that, Mr. Law.

148. INT. CHARLEY MOLEMAN'S — NIGHT

SILENT IMAGE: Gangster-like in hat, suit and tie, Robert plays
guitar hooked to a speaker with an electric pickup. Johnny plays
second guitar and Calvin, wrist bandaged, plays drums. Bold
letters on the bass drum spell "ROBERT JOHNSON."

Panic strikes the dancing joint as cops raid with clubs and guns. Women strip naked as the lights go out and, their black bodies camouflaged, they flee into the blackness.

> LAW (O.S.)
>
> Well, Bob, I wish you all the luck in the world. Now do let us know exactly where you'll be so your royalties can reach you right away. In any case, it's been a pleasure. Perhaps we'll meet again, God willing.

149. EXT. CHARLEY MOLEMAN'S — NIGHT

SILENT IMAGE: The cops have set the place ablaze and escape in their cars. Robert, leaving his friends behind a tree, runs to the burning joint and bravely peers inside.

Through a window we see Robert's wired guitar leaning on a chair, in flames. Johnny's is destroyed. When the bass drum catches fire, the "ROBERT JOHNSON" logo perishes.

Footsteps in the studio, then the closing of a door.

150. EXT. ROAD NEAR CHARLEY MOLEMAN'S — LATE NIGHT

SILENT IMAGE: Robert runs to the paved road by the blazing joint. He wails away on blues harp, performing a sensational tap dance as cars veer to the roadside. Silvery coins shower Robert as he dances in the headlights.

DISSOLVE TO

151. EXT. WOODLAND — LATE NIGHT

FADE IN SOUND: Flipping a coin as he steps through a row of fallen trees, Robert passes a moonlit stand of pines adorned by ropes descending gracefully from each treetop.

152. EXT. HOUSE PARTY — NIGHT

A clapboard house by a fallow field. A banner over the porch reads "GETBACK."

SUPER: Near Three Forks, Mississippi, August 1938

People move about as Robert sings "Little Queen of Spades."

> ROBERT (O.S.)
>
> *She the li'l Queen of Spades, an' she will not let me be /*
> *Whene'er she make a spread oo! cold chill run over me—*

RALPH drags his broken Victrola beneath the "GETBACK" banner and places it outside on the porch.

153. INT. HOUSE PARTY — NIGHT

Robert keeps everyone dancing. Particularly sinuous LOUISE.

> ROBERT
>
> *I'm gonna get me a gamblin' woman, if that's the last*
> *thing that I do / A man don't need a woman—hoo fair*
> *brown!—he got to give all his money to—*

Louise shimmies over to Robert and rubs her butt on his arm. He pokes his guitar neck at the tempting target.

154. EXT. PORCH — NIGHT

Louise's husband Ralph works on the Victrola with a screwdriver.

> ROBERT (O.S.)
>
> *Everybody says she got a mojo, 'cause she been usin' that*
> *stuff / But she got a way of trimmin' down—hoooo!—*
> *an' I mean it's most too tough—*

Ralph looks in the window. The party is a success, with his wife, stroking Robert's head, enjoying it most of all.

155. INT. HOUSE PARTY — NIGHT

Robert sings for Louise as the drunken atmosphere heightens. She rubs her groin on seated Robert's shoulder.

> ROBERT
>
> *Li'l girl I am a king, an' fair brown you is a queen /*
> *Let's put our heads together so's we can make our money*
> *green—*

Ralph beholds the scene from the door. When Robert sticks his empty whiskey bottle into Louise's mouth, Ralph grips his screwdriver and heads for a nearby shed.

156. INT. TOOL SHED — NIGHT

Ralph patiently examines a few wrenches and screwdrivers. He selects one of each, then takes down a small glass bottle of "Black Spider" crop poison and pockets it.

157. INT. HOUSE PARTY — NIGHT

Robert performs the discordant masterpiece "Hellhound on My Trail" as Louise pets him.

> ROBERT
>
> *I got to keep movin', got to keep movin' / Blues fallin'*
> *down like hail / An' the day keeps on 'mindin' me,*
> *there's a hellhound on my trail—*

Ralph strolls back through and goes out the door, casually glancing at the dancing and his wanton wife.

158. **EXT. PORCH — NIGHT**

Ralph carries a soda bottle filled with whiskey to the Victrola, then furtively adds the poison. Louise steps out and puts her arm around him as he kneels to fix the Victrola.

> LOUISE
>
> Ralph, honey, why ain't you inside dancing with me? How come, baby?

> RALPH
>
> Gotta fix this for ya first, doll. I can't dance anyways. You know me.

> LOUISE
>
> Can't dance? Since when? That boy inside make anyone dance!

> RALPH
>
> We do our dancin' in bed. Here now, bring that li'l sissy somethin' to drink. He earned it. An' don't be worryin' 'bout me none.

Louise kisses Ralph and reenters the house.

> ROBERT (O.S.)
>
> *Now if today was Christmas Eve, an' tomorrow was Christmas Day—*

SEEN THROUGH A WINDOW, Robert takes the bottle from Louise and drinks up while playing for her.

> ROBERT (SPOKEN)
>
> Aw, wouldn't we have a time, baby!

159. **INT. HOUSE PARTY — LATE NIGHT**

Louise lifts her skirt up her thighs for Robert.

ROBERT

*All's I need's my li'l sweet rider, just to pass the time
away, uh-huh / To pass the time away—*

Robert smiles at her tentatively, wincing, bothered by something
unclear to him. She tries to dance with him but, pain-wracked,
Robert can't.

160. **EXT. PORCH — LATE NIGHT**

Ralph sees the empty bottle by unsteady Robert's feet.

ROBERT

*You sprinkled hot foot powder all around your daddy's
door / Keeps me with ramblin' in mind, every ol' place
I go—*

He calmly returns to the Victrola as Louise walks over.

LOUISE

C'mon, darlin', party's gonna be over soon. That boy's
about had it.

RALPH

We paid him good—he ain't done yet. You go on
back. I be in a minute.

She ducks inside as Ralph lugs the Victrola after her.

ROBERT

*I can tell the wind is risin', leaves tremblin' on the tree /
All I need's my li'l sweet woman, to keep me company,
keep me—keep me—kee—*

161. EXT. HOUSE PARTY — WEE HOURS

Abruptly Robert bangs backward out the door and, tossing his guitar, tumbles off the porch. The guests pour out to find him yelping like a rabid animal, kicking up clouds of dust.

Chased across the yard, he drops to hands and knees again in the billowing dust. Raising his bottle in tribute behind him, the devilman smiles and scratches his balls as Lavendar taunts Robert, jumping for joy on two good legs.

> LAVENDAR
>
> KNEEEE HIIIIGH!!!!

Robert scampers like a dog on all fours into the field as Ralph and Louise embrace in a window nearby. He stands and collapses, alone.

162. EXT. COTTON FIELD — MORNING

A hundred yards away, two SHARECROPPERS stroll in from the field as an unidentifiable third sharecropper tends to fallen Robert.

> CROPPER 1
>
> Who the debil done it?

> CROPPER 2
>
> Lyons, like before.

> CROPPER 1
>
> Willie 'gain?

Behind them the unidentifiable man drags Robert from the field.

> CROPPER 2

Yeah. Got 'im to his hand an' knee an' stab 'im. Cut open all his ches? My rider an' me, we seen it. Boy from Hazlehurst—

163. INT. ONE-ROOM SHACK — NOON

Resting in a small room with sagging painted wallpaper, patched with newspaper, Robert's convulsions are feeble now. Seated at his feet by a radio, drinking, is the devilman.

> ROBERT

How—how long I been here?

The devilman looks away. He drinks, then he eyes Robert.

> ROBERT

Where's the doctor? When he come?

The devilman swigs his bottle and fiddles with the radio.

> ROBERT

What's yo' name?

> DEVILMAN

Tush Hogg. Doctor Tush Hogg.

> ROBERT

That ain't it.

> DEVILMAN

Then what is.

ROBERT

Gimme a paper. I'll tell you.

The devilman hands him a slip of paper, steps to the door and flags down a white pickup truck. He sees Robert drop the pencil, dead. The devilman reads the slip of paper.

SLIP OF PAPER: "Jesus Christ my saver an redeemer"

164. EXT. ONE ROOM SHACK — NOON

The devilman lays Robert on the pickup's rear bed as Washington Phillips's sublime "I Had a Good Father and Mother" plays. It is the most beautiful song in the film.

SUPER: At the time of the murder, Don Law was searching for Robert Johnson throughout Mississippi, with an offer for him to sing in New York City at Carnegie Hall. But on August 16, 1938, Robert Johnson died and was buried somewhere in the Delta in an unmarked grave.

The pickup truck drives down the dusty road with the lifeless body of Robert Johnson shifting about behind.

RECORDING

I'm so glad Salvation is free, it is free for you and me /
Now if we only live with Jesus how happy we could be—

The melody heightens into a magically precious cooing, as the distant truck disappears in its own clouds of dust.

DISSOLVE TO

165. PHOTOGRAPH OF ROBERT JOHNSON

A studio photograph of Robert Johnson, wearing a new suit and fedora, battered guitar on his lap. He's smiling innocently, tentatively, leaning forward slightly, his faraway eyes staring downward in different directions.

RECORDING

I know this whole round world don't love me no how, an' it is on the count of sin / But I'm so thankful God is able to give me many friends—

SUPER: THE END

Robert Johnson studio portrait. Hooks Bros., Memphis, circa 1935.
© 1989 Delta Haze Corporation. All rights reserved. Used by permission.

"Jake's Place," a jook joint lost in the fields between Morgan City and Itta Bena, Mississippi, near Three Forks, where Robert Johnson last played. Interior walls were painted randomly in different dark shades, with a polka-dotted ceiling, larger-than-life carnal images, and a sign reading "No bad language, please."

A tiny white clapboard Baptist church on the edge of a cottonfield, shaded by a chinaberry tree, six miles north of Clarksdale, Mississippi. It was razed in 1980. The local voodoo conjurer kept his office in back inside the church. *"Good with two magics better than one—"*

A crossroads on Charlie's Trace, a shortcut between a Mississippi River landing and the hills, a few miles below Clarksdale. This dirt swath, allegedly cut by a Choctaw Indian, was the route of marauding outlaws in the early 1800s and of itinerant bluesmen in the early 1900s.

In Friars Point, Mississippi, Alan Greenberg was referred to Dutch Carter, a ninety-three-year-old former bartender with vivid memories of his friend Charley Patton. When approached, the man said he wasn't Dutch Carter and hadn't heard of him. Two days later, after learning of his visitor's purpose from people in town, he changed his mind and generously provided his recollections of 1930s riverside jook and barrelhouses. Then he was asked why he had first denied being Dutch Carter. "That's the problem," he complained. "Since I come here forty years ago, everyone calls me Dutch Carter. But my name's Willie McGee."

Fringed by dark trees on tufted banks, the Sunflower River winds through Clarksdale, a typical Delta town with flat terrain, far horizons, and vast surrounding cottonfields. The former cotton processing and musical hub is now the home of the Delta Blues Museum.

Levees were notorious for shielding not only riverside towns from flood tides but criminals and "sinners" from the forces of law and morality. On the far side of the levee, every sort of character acted out his darkest fantasies in an atmosphere of sinister, oblivious dread. Insipid attempts to control ways of the soul resulted in warning signs like this one on the levee road near Friars Point.

A cobblestoned street and storefronts (scarcely changed since the early 1900s, like many Delta towns) beside the railroad tracks in Itta Bena. Bluesmen were often encouraged to perform outside these local shops to attract customers. But due to the Mississippi "dry state" laws, which supplanted the repealed national statute prohibiting hard liquor after 1933, a liquor store such as this one would not have been in business back in Robert Johnson's day.

With its stark skeletal cypresses and weeping willows, the Yazoo River (Choctaw for "River of Death") starts near Greenwood and runs along U.S. Highway 61 to Redwood, where it diverges and ceases its flow just north of Vicksburg.

NOTES

[1]

1. "During a peaceful lull in the Afro-American church service, after a song has been sung and the church is resting, or after the deacon has prayed and led the first hymn and everyone sits wondering what will come, then an ethereal humming arises among the women: the *Lining Hymn*, or the *Church-House Moan*. A spiritual pure and ineffable, the strong, sorrowful moan moves through the room like an ancestral breeze stirring placid waters. An older woman in the rear starts tapping a quick staccato rhythm with her toe to set the tempo for all that follows. The deacon and congregation adorn the air with unexpected harmonies as the minister leans forward and, in a deep despairing voice that tugs at the heart, raises the first line of his sermon." Alan Lomax, *Recorded Anthology of American Music* (New York: New World Records, 1977), liner notes.

2. A vanishing custom among Southern Afro-American people. By swinging the ax through the threatening winds or using it to chop up the ground, one is able then to "chop the storm in two" and so stop it. Others stick a blade in the ground to "split the cloud," or simply place an ax in a corner of the house. "The use of the ax as an antidote to the storm

is significant, since the West African god of thunder and lightning, *Shango*, is an ax." What has survived is folk custom, devoid of African theological background, reenacting an original mythological image. Albert J. Raboteau, *Slave Religion* (New York: Oxford, 1978), 81.

3. "SUPER" is a shortened form of "superimposition," in this case referring to the appearance of text over the visual image.

4. While his mother and second stepfather Willie "Dusty" Willis labored on the Abbay-Leatherman plantation in nearby Commerce, Robert Johnson grew to manhood in and around Robinsonville, a small (population 150) Mississippi cotton community forty miles south of Memphis. Enrolled under his first stepfather's pseudonym of Spencer at the Indian Creek School in Commerce, Robert learned the identity of his natural father—one of his mother's lovers—and began to introduce himself as Robert *Johnson*. There were four *jook joints* (see below) in the Robinsonville area, where Robert would steal away with his Jew's harp or harmonica to listen to Willie Brown, Charley Patton, Ernest "Whisky Red" Brown, and, upon his arrival in June 1930, Eddie "Son" House.

[2]

1. Friars Point (population 988 in 1930), sitting in the shadow of a flood wall blocking the Mississippi River from view, was abandoned as a county seat in 1930 because of the menacing river, which had swallowed every major river town established since 1830. A forsaken community today, old-timers gather outside a dry goods store to fill the desolate air with recollected images of traveling singers from W. C. Handy to Charley Patton, those native and adopted sons who once drew masses of delighted black folk and tolerant whites to local street corners half a century ago. Few of the

living express any concern or need for the African home-
land; fewer still remember their elders' reflections, told as
truth with touches of fantasy, documenting remedies for the
repressed horrors of spiritual displacement.

2. Willie Johnson was a singer of religious songs from Mar-
lin, Texas, who, like several of his contemporaries, was as-
signed the nickname "Blind" for his recordings and came
to be known as Blind Willie Johnson. His songs, even when
taken from hymnals, were profoundly expressive of his personal poetic vision, with a vibrancy of tone and a vividness
of image. On a farm near the Brazos River where he was
born around 1902, Willie's stepmother threw a pan of lye in
his face when he was seven to get even with his father for a
beating, thereby leaving the boy sightless for life. He sang in
the streets of small cotton towns in southern Texas and came
to Dallas in 1927, where his future wife and singing partner
Angeline followed him as he sang "If I Had My Way I'd Tear
This Building Down" until he noticed her. Sounding like
a man many years older than he was, Willie rendered his
first recordings in Dallas that same year and became one of
the most successful recording artists in the South for several
years. When his record company went bankrupt in 1932, he
dropped from sight and never recorded again. Caught one
night in 1949 in a house fire in Beaumont, Texas, he and
Angeline managed to douse the flames and then, having
no money to go elsewhere, they climbed back into their
charred, drenched bed and went to sleep. Willie soon came
down with pneumonia while continuing to sing on the
chilly streets. When he finally sought help at a local hospital, he was told that no blind people were allowed in, so he
returned to his devastated home and died within days. Some
of Blind Willie Johnson's most beloved songs were "Jesus
Make Up My Dying Bed," "Trouble Soon Be Over," "Lord, I
Just Can't Keep from Crying," "Motherless Children Have a

Hard Time," and "Nobody's Fault but Mine." Samuel Charters, *Blind Willie Johnson, 1927–1930* (New York: Folkways Records, 1965), liner notes.

3. Sharecroppers were tenant farmers in the racially corrupt agricultural system that dominated the South until the Afro-American diaspora of the 1930s and '40s. Kept helplessly compliant through official programs of economic and educational deprivation, the black sharecroppers wallowed in permanent debt, owing to imaginary, grossly inflated fees charged by white landowners. The blacks were wise to such cruelty but were powerless to do anything about it, outside of moving into urban industrial centers for a different sort of squalid self-mockery.

4. After a recollection offered by Shad Hall, Harold Courlander, *A Treasury of Afro-American Folklore* (New York: Crown Publishers, 1976).

[3]

1. *Jook joints*, sometimes called *barrelhouses*, as essential to the Afro-American reality in the Delta as the Church, sheltered the lunar visage of the Sunday religious service, the Saturday night dance. The word "jook" seems to be derived from any of several sources in West African culture, such as *joog*, which suggests "to agitate" or "shake up," or *yuka*, from the Vili Congo dialect, connoting "making a noise, to hit or beat." Typically no more than a primitive, one-room shanty, the jook would be found in some remote terrestrial zone far from the church and even further from the law (the bootlegger-proprietors often paid for police immunity). People went there to drink, dance, play or listen to music, gamble, look for a fight, look for a lover, and so on. Beer was served in tin cups, whiskey and gin in cans or the same tin cups; mugs weren't used "because the people would commit

mayhem, tear people's heads up with those things—rough places they were," reflects John Shines. "When you were playing in a place like that," Mr. Shines continues, "you just sit back there with the dancing on a cane-bottomed chair, just rear back and cut loose." Live music gradually disappeared from most Delta jooks with the advent of the jukebox, or *vendor*, but several jooks with live music may be found in northwestern Mississippi today, such as Jake's Place, a visionary sheet metal hovel lost in a cotton field somewhere south of Itta Bena.

2. Willie Brown was one of the greatest of Delta bluesmen. A brilliant, forceful guitarist, he is remembered for his accompaniment of Charley Patton and Son House, and for his recordings of "Future Blues" and "M & O Blues." Brown was born around the turn of the century and spent much of his life in Robinsonville, where he came into contact with Robert Johnson. Robert copied his mentor's exaggerated plucking technique but avoided Brown's tendency to break guitar strings. Listed as William Brown, he recorded for Alan Lomax and the Library of Congress in 1942 and may be heard today on album AFS L59.

3. Eddie "Son" House was born near Riverton, Mississippi, in 1898, and was raised across the river from Vicksburg in Louisiana. He was brought up "in church," in opposition to the Devil-courting bluesmen and their followers. "It always made me mad to see a man with a guitar, singing these blues and things," he reflected many years later. House became one of the most powerful and emotional singers in the Delta, working regularly with the likes of Brown, Patton, and, later, Robert Johnson. His 1930 recordings of "Preachin' the Blues," "My Black Mama," and "Delta Blues" are monuments of the genre, as are his 1942 recordings of "Jinx Blues," "Special Rider Blues," and "Depot Blues" for the Library of Congress. After receiving but forty dollars from

his record company for his 1930 releases, and then just a bottle of Coca-Cola from Alan Lomax for his work in 1942, Son disappeared from view until the 1964 Newport Folk Festival, with his wealth of talent and spirit largely undiminished. He made a score of excellent new recordings before retiring once more, to Detroit this time, where he died in 1988.

4. In 1903, W. C. Handy was touring the Delta with his orchestra when, in the Mississippi town of Tutwiler, not far from Charley Patton's home in Drew, "a lean, loose-jointed Negro had commenced plucking a guitar beside me. . . . As he played, he pressed a knife on the strings of the guitar" and performed "the weirdest music" Handy had ever heard. This was the first documentation of slide or bottleneck guitar technique, an art form in itself today after generations of development by Delta, Hawaiian, and country-western guitar players. Using a blade, piece of pipe, glass bottle, or bone, the musician slides his tool up and down the guitar neck to bend and extend various chords or, in the parlance of the Southern Afro-American, to make the guitar *talk*. The technique is technically rather simple to learn, and Son House was a master slide guitarist by 1930, although he'd been too "churchified" to learn guitar at all until 1927, less than three years before.

5. Delta musicians would frequently expand the boundaries of a given song, or render it unidentifiable altogether, by interchanging verses and versions of different songs within the basic melodic-rhythmic structure of the original. This was done spontaneously, either in solo or group performance, and called for a mind like a deranged computer bank. Since a typical jook joint song performance often lasted twenty minutes or more (until a trancelike momentum had been achieved), a jook entertainer would be hard-pressed to please his demanding audience. Once a singer faltered, it wouldn't

be long before another singer challenged him to an improvisational duel on the spot, or simply replaced him.

6. In this scene, Son House and Willie Brown are depicted trading verses to different songs while performing the same song together. Son borrows from Charley Patton's "Screamin' and Hollerin' the Blues" ("Girl, my mama's gettin' old, her head is turnin' gray. / Don't you know it'll break her heart, know my livin' this-a-way?"), while Willie shouts out his own "M & O Blues" ("An' I asked her, 'How 'bout it?' Lord, an' she said, 'All right,' / But she never showed up at the shack last night . . ."").

[4]

1. Robert Johnson was a devilishly handsome Afro-American man with a markedly youthful mien who, according to accounts of those who knew him, almost always appeared meticulously groomed. John Shines, who traveled extensively with Robert for a few weeks prior to Robert's death, recollected, "We'd be on the road for days and days, no money and sometimes not much food, let alone a decent place to spend the night, playing on dusty streets or inside dirty places of the sort you played in in those times, and as I'd catch my breath and see myself looking like a *dog*, there'd be Robert, all clean as can be, looking like he's just stepped out of *church*. Never did nothing to himself any more than me, neither."

2. *Hootch* was one of several slang terms for illegally distilled corn whiskey sold throughout the Delta and elsewhere. In 1930 the popularity of various types of bootleg liquor among Southern black people was due not so much to federal Prohibition but rather to the Mississippi "dry state" laws, which supplanted the repealed national statute against hard liquor after 1933.

3. Goat is a character derived by the author from two people who actually lived and performed music in the South around the time of Robert Johnson. Essentially, this character is drawn from the remarkable singer and songwriter Tommy Johnson, who was born around 1896 in Terry, Mississippi, and died in 1956 in Crystal Springs, Mississippi. Recently established as a distant relative of Robert Johnson by his biographer David Evans, Tommy Johnson, a strange primitive genius, affected his generation of musicians more than anyone except Charley Patton. It was from Patton, in fact, that Johnson received his primary musical schooling, during the intense musical scene around the Drew, Mississippi, plantations from about 1912 to 1918. Johnson was famous for his wondrous vocal technique; instead of the customary chant, he *yodeled* several of his songs, swallowing his words to obliterate whatever literal value they might have had (which was the case with most Afro-American singers, who utilized their acquired language for *imaginal* ends, more than literal). However renowned he might have been for his music, Johnson was equally famous for his weird drinking habits. One of the greatest drunkards of all time, he would drink anything—denatured alcohol, shoe polish, petroleum extracts—anything that would get him high. Addicted to Sterno, a jellied cooking fuel, he drank several cans a day right up to his peaceful death at the age of sixty. "He believed in it," says his brother Mager. Johnson was alleged to have been an agent of the Devil, a rumor he encouraged to enhance his personal legend and popularity. Among the fifteen surviving Tommy Johnson songs on record ("Louisiana Blues" has never been found), the most celebrated are his "Canned Heat Blues," "Maggie Campbell Blues," "Big Road Blues," and the incomparable, hallucinatory "Cool Drink of Water." David Evans, *Tommy Johnson* (London: Studio Vista, 1971).

4. One of the many songs recorded during the 1930s on the "jake leg" theme. The emotionally urgent version by Poor Boy Lofton, sung here by Lavendar, documents the paralysis and other afflictions suffered by countless Delta black people who drank a bootlegged ginger extract as an inexpensive whiskey substitute. Also referred to as the "limber leg."

5. As a young boy, Robert Johnson would return from a day in the cotton fields, head down behind his stepfather's cart, his figure increasingly covered with dust. The inevitable nickname "Dusty"—a nemesis to Robert, being the tag worn by his second stepfather as well—followed.

6. Robert's mother, Julia Ann Majors, was married to Charles Dodds Jr., a well-respected farmer and landowner. A personal conflict with two powerful white businessmen forced Dodds to flee Mississippi for Memphis in 1907, where he assumed the name of Spencer. Julia stayed behind with two of her daughters in Hazlehurst. On May 8, 1911, Robert Johnson was born to Julia Dodds and Noah Johnson, a sharecropper with whom Julia had had an affair during her husband's enforced absence. Despite recent claims to the contrary, Johnny Shines and others who knew Robert assert that Robert never met his father, and from time to time swung between a sullen disregard for him and an obsessive concern for his whereabouts.

[6]

1. Willie is singing a verse from Son's "Jinx Blues," one of young Robert's favorites ("You know the blues ain't nothin' but a lowdown, shakin' achin' chill./ Well, if you ain't had 'em, honey, I hope you never will . . ."). Copyright 1965 by Sondick Music Company.

2. In his preadolescent years, while he was still known as Robert Spencer, Robert committed himself to music by taking up the Jew's harp. This instrument was soon replaced by the harmonica, which had been introduced to him by his best friend. Upon making the transition to guitar a few years later, Robert fashioned a rack for his harmonica out of string and baling wire, then worked out songs for his voice and instrumental accompaniment. Leroy Carr's "How Long, How Long Blues" was used early on as one of Robert's instructional models.

3. Eventually, Son prevented such accidents by wrapping an oily rag around his hand for protection from the sharp glass bottleneck.

[8]

1. Charley Patton was the pre-eminent Delta bluesman of his day, a man whose shamanistic spirit and ways defined his musical idiom aesthetically and culturally, and encouraged its growth. Born near Edwards, Mississippi, in 1891, Patton was almost a generation older than most of his contemporaries. Physically small, he was a strange-looking blend of white, black, but primarily Indian blood; dressed like an urchin in his snug suit and bow tie, Patton seemed to be a Rimbaudian image incarnate or, from another angle, "he looked kind of like a Puerto Rican," according to Howlin' Wolf. "He was illiterate, and spent his time in total idleness, inevitably drunk. His friends remember him as a troublemaker, a runt with a big mouth and quick feet. Patton was extremely cheap with whatever money he had, would pledge eternal love to any woman gullible enough to listen, and was a notorious tyrant with his eight-odd common-law wives, beating them regularly. Since he was a favorite with the whites as well as the blacks, Patton passed easily

between antipodal worlds while hardly ever putting in an honest day's labor. 'That's the way he lived, eating out of the white folks' kitchen,' says Son House. He must have been the very archetype of the 'bad plantation nigger' around the Will Dockery and Joe Kirby plantations, where he spent most of his time. His only child, China Lu, disavowed him.

"Patton's hoard of imitators all lacked some of his virtues. No one compared with him for colorful, exciting and shamelessly lewd public performances, nor did any of his musical peers leave so extensive a studio portrait. His repertoire was broader than the typical Mississippian's, encompassing hard Delta blues, ragtime, 'covers' of popular songs, and folk blues or ballads. His crude lyricism offers local-color imagery unmatched by any other bluesman. His diction and vocal techniques were so unusual and idiosyncratic that purists like Son House scorned him for rendering his songs unintelligible," which they probably were when sung most successfully. Although Patton's music indicates a good grasp of melody and harmony, his genius was principally rhythmic, with rhythm assuming such importance in each work that it ultimately became the work itself. Owing to the nature of his singing rhythms, Patton's guitar instrumentation took on the cadence of speech, most notably so in "Spoonful," one of his landmark recordings. Other great recordings of his are "Pony Blues," "Tom Rushen Blues," "Some These Days I'll Be Gone," "High Water Everywhere," and "Pea Vine Blues." He also recorded religious songs, under the pseudonym of Elder J. J. Hadley. Three months after recording with his wife Bertha Lee in New York City, Charley Patton died in Holly Ridge, Mississippi, of heart failure. Nick Perls, Stephen Calt, et al., *Charley Patton—Founder of the Delta Blues* (New York: Yazoo Records, L-1020), liner notes. John Fahey, *Charley Patton* (London: Studio Vista, 1970).

[10]

1. "Long, Hot Summer Days" is a work song recorded in Texas in 1939 by John A. and Ruby T. Lomax. Sung in the fields by Clyde Hill and his fellow prisoners at Clemens State Farm in Brazoria, this recording can be found on a Library of Congress LP, AFS L3.

2. The only people to accompany Charley Patton on record were his wife Bertha Lee (see note 28:1), Willie Brown, and the Clarksdale fiddler Henry Sims. Sims, who later recorded for the Library of Congress with Muddy Waters, was an articulate primitive on fiddle who complemented Patton perfectly. The rough tones of Sims's inimitable fiddle are due to his instrument being homemade, or in an absurd state of disrepair. As a singer he possessed a distinctly mournful quality, which went well with his playing. Among his recordings are "Farrell Blues," "Come Back Corrina," "Tell Me Man Blues," and "Be True Be True Blues," all with a drunken Charley Patton in dubious support. Don Kent, *Patton, Sims, and Bertha Lee* (New York: Herwin Records, 1977), liner notes.

3. H. C. Speir was the white owner of a Jackson music store who acted as a talent scout for the major record companies in the "race" and "hillbilly" markets. He would find artists who were already popular in the black community, make test recordings of them in his store, send these to the companies for approval, and then make the arrangements for the accepted artists to get to the studios to record. Born in Mississippi in 1895, Speir grew up liking the black music he heard all around him, which helped make his taste quite close to the black audiences of his day. His sole criterion for selecting a good singer was his personal taste, not the singer's popularity among blacks. Speir claimed he never could tell a good blues singer, as some sounded excellent in person

but poor on record, or vice versa. He was also unaware that many blues lyrics were metaphorical, and took all the songs he heard at face value. Speir was a friendly man who was interested in music as much for pleasure as for profit. The Jackson area's finest musicians would frequent his store to buy strings and picks, or just chat. Some of the musicians who came to Speir's store and were "discovered" by Speir were Tommy Johnson, Charley Patton, Willie Brown, Skip James, and Ishman Bracey. Evans, *Tommy Johnson*, 45–46.

4. "This Old World's in a Hell of a Fix" was the subject of a sermon given by Rev. Dr. J. McPherson, also known as Black Billy Sunday, in 1931.

[11]

1. Goat is singing Tommy Johnson's extraordinary "Cool Drink of Water." The verses of the song are disconnected but traditional, and can be found scattered among many other country blues performances. The music of the song is startling. Almost half of the vocal, including the "Lord, Lordy Lord" primal refrain, is sung in falsetto, creating the overall impression of a chant somewhere in between a field holler and an Alpine yodel. Yet the instrumentation is unique and quite sophisticated, with the guitars perfectly integrated into the vocal line. The 1928 recording was released on Victor 21279. Evans, *Tommy Johnson*, 48–49.

2. An Afro-American spiritual dating back to the days of slavery, recently recorded for cultures worldwide by the Rolling Stones.

[12]

1. After his 1928 recording session Tommy Johnson never recorded again. His records were popular and sold very well,

but a strange misunderstanding coupled with Johnson's per-
petual drunkenness ended his recording career. What apparently happened was this: the Mississippi Sheiks recorded a
song taken from Johnson's own "Big Road Blues" and made
an enormous hit out of it. The Victor Company, which
owned "Big Road Blues," sued the Okeh Company, which
recorded the Sheiks, and a settlement was made. Johnson,
the composer of the song, was included in the settlement,
but he was drunk at the time and wound up with less than
he deserved. And somehow he believed that he had sold his
right to record ever again. His brother thought the same
thing. "He drank so much he sold his rights, and he couldn't
put out no more records," said the Rev. LeDell Johnson.
"According to his records he didn't get nothing much. See,
when Tom get broke, he would sell anything to get a drink
of whisky or a drink of alcorub or anything that'd bring on
drunk." Evans, *Tommy Johnson*, 68.

[16]

1. A vestige of Afro-American slavery days and, then again, of
    ancestral times in the African homeland, the *one-string* is
    the most primitive musical instrument associated with the
    Delta blues. Whether constructed for portability from a dis-
    carded two-by-four or simply nailed to a wall, the one-string
    is made with a steel wire strung between two nails three feet
    apart and raised above the two-by-four or wall by bridges;
    one bridge is a stone or wooden block, the other a hollow
    vial or pill bottle fastened beneath a resonator fashioned
    from an empty paint can. The player of the instrument beats
    the wire near the resonator with a whittled stick while slid-
    ing a half-pint whiskey flask up and down the wire to al-
    ter tones. Plucking is often used in place of the percussion.
    Frederick Usher, *One-String Blues* (Santa Monica: Takoma
    Records, 1960), liner notes.

2. The Piney Woods of Mississippi is an irregular triangle of forest land whose landscape of stumps, ghost towns left by the lumber trade, and hastily reforested tracts tell its story. Until lumbering built a few fair-sized towns out of the wilderness it was a pioneer territory; by 1930, with the woods ravaged and the poorly built mill houses rotting, it had become pioneer country once more. Like all pioneers, the Afro-American people of the Piney Woods were economically poor, politically unpredictable, and in a constant state of transition. With the geographic and economic character of the region losing its meaning among its inhabitants, the Piney Woods assumed an ill-defined but widespread mythical character. Federal Writers' Project, Works Progress Administration, *Mississippi—A Guide to the Magnolia State* (New York: Hastings House, 1938), 6.

[18]

1. Five miles west on the graveled road from Robinsonville, Commerce (population 50 in 1930) was once a rival of Memphis for the river trade before becoming a plantation anchored by the big house built upon a large Indian burial mound. Richard Abbay first bought the land from the Chickasaw tribe in 1832, but the ravenous Mississippi flood tide destroyed the settlement by the time of the Civil War. The rebuilt Abbay-Leatherman plantation bordered both sides of the road from Robinsonville with its commissaries and planted fields. The main house was not constructed directly upon the Indian mound because of the owner's aversion to touching a mound "full of the dead." From the top of the mound, which rises now behind the house, De Soto had his first glimpse of the river that was to be his grave, in 1541. Federal Writer's Project, *Mississippi*, 316.

2. Lonnie Johnson was one of the first blues guitarists to achieve commercial stardom. His work bordered on jazz,

and he was comfortable within each idiom. Born in New Orleans, probably in 1894, Johnson first achieved proficiency on the violin before he took up the guitar in 1917. He was an immediate success upon the release of his first recordings in 1926; by the time the Depression ended the first phase of his recording career in 1932, Johnson had produced 130 sides, more than any male blues singer of the period. His fame was unparalleled within the blues universe, and his influence on other musicians was very pronounced. Young Robert Johnson not only bore the Lonnie Johnson imprint on guitar but was known to go around claiming kinship to the star. Long interpreted as idiosyncratic evidence of his egotistical nature, Robert's claims concerning the older musician have been corroborated recently by researchers.

3. And, conversely, Son House learned the main tricks on Robert Johnson. The younger man's ultimate influence on his "mentor" House is generally overlooked.

4. In truth, Robert did not make any commercial recordings of any kind until November 1936.

5. Scrapper Blackwell, born Francis Black, was a celebrated black recording artist known for his brilliant guitarmanship, particularly in tandem with his equally celebrated partner, Leroy Carr.

[19]

1. The shimmy-she-wa-wa was a popular dance of the period. "They did that some way like that, you know, with their knees," remembers the Rev. Rubin Lacy, a bluesman once himself. "That's the reason I say it's all coming back. Ain't nothing but what you see them do now: whole lot of shaking going on." Evans, *Tommy Johnson*, 40.

[20]

1. "There's No Use Lovin,'" one of Lonnie Johnson's earliest re-
    cordings (1926). Johnson plays the piano here, occasionally
    giving way to a whining siren. On Mamlish Records, num-
    ber S-3807.

[21]

1. Moon Lake, located two and a half miles west of Lula, Mis-
    sissippi (see scene 85).

[22]

1. Taken from the woodcarved epitaph of an unknown slave.
    Harold Courlander, *A Treasury of Afro-American Folklore*
    (New York: Crown Publishers, 1976), 280.

2. Ike Zinnerman was a friend of Robert Johnson's from Grady,
    Alabama, who spent many a night teaching the younger
    man (in reality, only a few years separated them) blues gui-
    tar techniques. Born at the turn of the century, Zinnerman
    claimed that he mastered the guitar in a "boneyard" at mid-
    night while sitting atop tombstones. Robert accompanied
    the bluesman before developing confidence enough to per-
    form alone.

3. Erich Neumann, *The Origins and History of Consciousness*
    (Princeton, N.J.: Princeton University Press, 1954), 159. A
    literal instance of the essentially mythological character of
    Robert Johnson's life experiences and fate.

4. "Shorty George" is a traditional folk blues motif sung by
    black inmates on the Southwestern and Southern penal
    farms. The title is derived from a slang term given the train
    that brings the prisoners' family, friends, and female visitors

from the outside world. The version familiar to the author was sung by Smith Casey in 1939 at the Clemens State Farm in Brazoria, Texas, as a dirge for a dead comrade. The rest of the song is as follows:

> *Yes, he died on the road,*
> *Yes, he died on the road,*
> *Had no money to pay his boa'd.*
> *Ahhhhhhhh, he was a friend of mine,*
> *Yes, he was a friend of mine;*
> *Every time I think now, just can't keep from cryin'.*
> *I . . . . I stole away an' cried,*
> *Yes, stole away an' cried;*
> *Never had no money, now I wasn't satisfied.*
> *Mmmmmmmmmmm, wonder what's the matter now?*
> *Lord, what is the matter now? . . .*

Recorded for the Library of Congress by John A. and Ruby T. Lomax, and found on LP AFS L4.

[23]

1. Abstract spiritual systems find manifold ways to work on a human being's naked soul. In moments of weakness or personal stress, blues singers were particularly susceptible to fits of guilt in their shadowy corner of the Baptist subculture. Incidents such as the one occurring here in Ike's shack were not so uncommon, perhaps, to Delta life.

[25]

1. From the Tennessee border to the north, to the Louisiana line along the southern end, U. S. Highway 61 runs the entire length of 335 miles between Mississippi's state lines. It passes through the state's great alluvial plain, the extensive flat land colloquially known as the Delta, with its sluggish

rivers, lakes, and bayous. During the nineteenth century slave ships landed near Natchez to deposit their human cargo for processing; the Africans were fed, clothed, and taught a few English words, then they were sold on a block that stood on what is now US 61. During the 1930s the cotton and lumber industries made good use of the thoroughfare, which connected major trading centers such as Memphis, Clarksdale, Vicksburg, Natchez, and Baton Rouge. Once emptied of their load, transport trucks would pick up sharecroppers needing a ride to town or the next plantation.

[28]

1. Bertha Lee Pate, later Bertha Lee Joiner, was the last of Charley Patton's common-law wives. She joined Patton sometime after his 1929 recording sessions and, despite a minimum of natural singing skills, she performed with him regularly until his death in 1934. When Patton's own skills were in rapid decline, she went with him to New York City for his last sessions and cut a few records of her own: "Yellow Bee," "Mind Reader Blues," "Oh, Death" and "Troubled 'Bout My Mother." When interviewed for information about her legendary husband years after his death, Bertha Lee remembered only that Charley Patton played the guitar. She died in 1975 at the age of seventy-three. Fahey, *Charley Patton*, 16. Kent, *Patton, Sims, and Bertha Lee*, liner notes.

2. "Shake It and Break It" seems to have come out of the ragtime tradition, being similar to Bill Moore's "Barbershop Rag." The Rev. Gary Davis recorded a version of the song much closer to its ragtime roots, while Walter "Buddy Boy" Hawkins (see scene 103) stayed closer to Patton's interpretation with his "Snatch It and Grab It," recorded with a soused Patton narrating the performance in the background.

[30]

1. *Conjure* is a theoretical and practical system stemming from African and Afro-American culture that makes sense of the mysterious and inexplicable occurrences of life. Like Christianity, conjure is a system of belief, a way of perceiving the world so that people are placed in the context of another world no less "real" than the ordinary one. Both attempt to locate the cause of irrational suffering. Not only is conjure a theory for explaining the mysteries of evil, but it is a practice as well for doing something about it. Because the conjuror has the power to "fix" and to remove "fixes," to harm and to cure, it is possible to locate the source of misfortune and control it. Thus the conjuror, as a man of power, has enjoyed since slavery a measure of authority in the Afro-American community directly proportional to belief in his power. Certain conjurors are known to have offices in various churches around the Mississippi Delta to this day. Raboteau, *Slave Religion*, 275–88.

2. The efficiency of the conjuror is rooted in his ability to "charm" his client or to counteract another charm. The nature of such charismatic power is manifested physically by various *hands* or *mojos* selected or devised by the conjuror, whose stock in trade includes pins, bones, bottles, reptiles, insects, horsehair, roots, and herbs. Graveyard dirt is considered particularly potent. It is also believed that each charm possesses a spirit. Consequently, some charms are moistened with liquor to strengthen their power by strengthening their spirits.

[31]

1. According to John Shines, Robert was an avid moviegoer who favored westerns and Clark Gable pictures.

[32]

1. Charlie's Trace, a dirt swath cut through fields and wilderness a few miles below Clarksdale, is alleged to have been made by a Choctaw Indian. The trail was a shortcut from Sunflower Landing on the Mississippi River to a spot in the hills twelve miles south of Charleston, Mississippi. It was often the route of outlaws who marauded through this region in the early 1800s.

[33]

1. Blind Lemon Jefferson was born in the summer of 1897 in Couchman, Texas, about seventy-five miles from Dallas. He was born blind and, denied an education, was forced to earn a living early on as an itinerant singer. After playing and singing on the streets of nearby Wortham, he started his lifelong travels, and by the time he was twenty Lemon was singing for country dances and parties throughout the South. Before the start of World War I, he and Huddie Ledbetter (better known as Leadbelly) traveled and sang together in the Dallas area; Leadbelly went to prison and Lemon found local renown. At first, however, singing wasn't enough: he also wrestled for money in Dallas theaters, billed as a blind novelty wrestler. He did much of his singing in brothels, drinking and playing guitar all night until the right girl was writhing in his lap. In 1922 he married a woman named Roberta, and they had a son about two years later. By this time he'd gotten so fat that, when he played, the guitar would sit atop his stomach, propped beneath his chin. Mayo Williams, talent director for Paramount Records, brought Lemon to Chicago in 1925 for the first of many sessions. Although his records were a huge success, he received very little from Paramount for them. He stayed with the company

probably because Williams pimped for him; at the end of a session Williams would pay the dissolute blind man with a few dollars, a bottle of booze, and a prostitute. Lemon recorded over ninety sides for Paramount in three years, singing every kind of song. Never a blues specialist, by the time he began recording he'd cultivated a fluent and rather remarkable blues guitar style. He was among the most inventive lyricists in the blues genre as well. By 1930 he was the best-selling country blues singer of his time. Some of his most celebrated recordings were "Black Snake Moan," "Easy Rider Blues," "Piney Woods Money Mama," "Match Box Blues," "Jack o'Diamond Blues," "'Lectric Chair Blues," and the everlasting "See That My Grave Is Kept Clean." He recorded religious songs under the pseudonym Deacon L. J. Bates. Blind Lemon Jefferson's death is shrouded in mystery, having occurred apparently in 1930, when he froze to death on a street one night in Chicago. Todd Titon, *Early Downhome Blues* (Chicago: Univesity of Illinois Press, 1977), 114. Arnold S. Caplin, *Blind Lemon Jefferson–Son House* (New York: Biograph Records, 1972), liner notes. Samuel Charters, *The Country Blues* (New York: Da Capo, 1975), 57–72.

[35]

1. See note 32:1.

[38]

1. With the ravenous Mississippi River forever threatening the existence of life and property along its shores, flood walls known as *levees* were raised to stymie the tides. To build these levees, and to ensure their efficacy with constant inspection and repair, levee *camps* were established in the backwater region between the flood walls and the river. The camps were manned by the roughest of black men,

usually convicts from area prison farms, and they earned widespread notoriety for their sinister and oftentimes violent ways. On weekend nights the overworked laborers welcomed truckloads of women from the nearest towns, and they would play together until the work week began anew. Parties were held in canvas tents erected under the trees near the river, and local musicians would risk their lives to provide the entertainment.

2. The Afro-American music to be found in and around Mississippi is by no means limited to guitars, fiddles, and harmonicas. In the northwest corner of the state, traditional music is performed on such instruments as panpipes (or "quills"), kazoos (or "jazz horns"), trombones, saxophones, mandolins, and pianos. Most fascinating of all is the use of the fife and drum, which first came to light in 1942 when Alan Lomax recorded the Sid Hemphill band, a session of critical importance for the understanding of black music in the United States. The fife is played in combination with a bass drum and one or two snare drums, and it is made by burning holes in stalks of cane cut from a creek bottom. It is not customary for more than one fife to be played at a time, and sometimes it is used as a solo instrument. The overwhelming influence on this type of music is African. A prominent trait is the emphasis on percussion; there is even a trace of a most vital function of African percussion, the *talking drum*. David Evans, *Afro-American Folk Music from Tate and Panola Counties, Mississippi* (Washington, D.C.: Library of Congress, Music Division, AFS L67, 1978), descriptive brochure.

3. Robert Johnson was known to carry a little black book with him for several years, using it to record whatever lyrics or ideas he might hear or have in mind. He could have picked this up from his friend Ike Zinnerman.

[40]

1. Son is singing verses from his "Preachin' the Blues Part 1" and "Preachin' the Blues Part 2." Caplin, *Blind Lemon Jefferson–Son House*, song lyrics.

2. According to Son House, "I Can Make My Own Songs," *Sing Out*, July 1965.

3. This may or may not have been a song performed by Robert Johnson at the time of his "debut" in Robinsonville; its title and lyrics do link it to Son House, circa 1931. This was the only one of Robert's songs to have a secondary title on file with the American Record Company, "Up Jumped the Devil." The original recording can be found on the Columbia Records LP *Robert Johnson, King of the Delta Blues Singers*, CL 1654.

[41]

1. According to Son House, "I Can Make My Own Songs."

[44]

1. Any white plantation owner was known among his tenant and itinerant laborers as the "Boss," the "bossman" or the "Big Boss," of which only the term "bossman" indicates any sort of friendly respect. The plantation system was so rigid, so solid and the owners' authority so complete, that the blacks came to use the term "bossman" to represent oppressive white society and law in general.

[45]

1. Recipe provided by Evans, *Tommy Johnson*, 57.

[46]

1. R. D. Norwood, known as "Peg Leg Sam" or "One-Legged Sam," was born in Crystal Springs, Mississippi, in the early 1890s and was living in Jackson by 1920. He played mandolin and guitar and was regarded more highly as an accompanist than as a singer. He was one of the men Tommy Johnson played with most in the early and mid-1920s. They fought a lot, too, according to the Rev. Ishmon Bracey. "A fellow we called One-Legged Sam used to play with us accompaniment. He would all the time jump on Tommy till I'd be around. He'd beat Tommy if he didn't do like he wanted him to do. He'd jump on him. He was trouble. Had one leg. He'd stand back talking with one of them crutches and before you know anything, he done knocked you down with one of 'em. He done killed two or three men with guns, knives, razors. He's just trouble. But I'm the onliest one that conquered him. Tommy wouldn't fight." Norwood moved to Chicago in 1932, where he played and recorded until his death in 1967. Evans, *Tommy Johnson*, 88.

[47]

1. Isaiah 24:1.

[49]

1. In the Southern black patois, a distinction was made between *musicianers*, characterized so by their instrumental proficiency, and songsters, regarded more for their singing and songwriting capabilities.

2. Black Mississippians often refer to Alabama as a Land of Death in personal conversation, storytelling, and song lyrics (see Charley Patton singing "Going to Move to Alabama,"

scene 78). The reverse attitude seems to be true as well. John Shines, who lived a few miles from the Mississippi border in Holt, Alabama, refused to set foot in Mississippi "because of the people"; he refused to do so for over thirty years.

3. James Hillman, *The Dream and the Underworld* (New York: Harper Colophon Books, 1979), 134.

4. Throughout the Delta, levees shielded not only the riverside from flood tides but "sinners" and criminals from the forces of morality as well. In the shadows or backwater woodlands or down on the dark riverbank, every sort of character imaginable acted out his blackest fantasies in an atmosphere of sinister, oblivious dread. People gambled, drank, did drugs, made love, murdered and played their favorite music most heartfully. The law could make only pathetic attempts to control such ways of the soul.

[50]

1. Robert Johnson, seventeen years old, married Virginia Travis, fifteen years old, in Penton, Mississippi, in February 1929.

2. The recordings left by Skip James are among the greatest in country blues and establish James as one of the few bluesmen of compositional genius. A proud if not arrogant man, he looked down upon popular music recording as a tool "to deaden the mind" and "make enemies of friends," but as a practitioner he prided himself for always sounding "kinda strange to the public." He saw singing as a means to support his stylish way of living. After his discovery by H. C. Speir (see note 10:3), James left by train in early 1931 for Paramount's Wisconsin studio in the deluded belief that this recording session was a prelude to Hollywood fame. After the session, Paramount officials assured him that he would make a "terrific hit" with the twenty-six songs he recorded,

inducing James to opt for deferred royalty payments as his records were issued. In 1932 he was on a breadline in Dallas, still awaiting checks for his last seven Paramount releases. When he threatened to sue, Paramount informed him of its decision to liquidate, a bitter disappointment that forced James out of the music business ("a barrel of crabs") for more than thirty years. He reverted to the part of "a plain, ordinary Skip," performing plantation labor instead of chanting other-worldly melodies, visionary laments. Ever compelled by the grandeur of success, James later characterized himself as "one of the star tractor drivers in Mississippi." Upon his strange reappearance at the 1964 Newport Folk Festival, it was evident that time had not eroded James's magnificent countertenor or his instrumental dexterity, but because of failing health he did not expect to live much longer. With almost perverse timing, the Cream rock 'n' roll band's version of his "I'm So Glad" became an international hit as he was succumbing to cancer. His death in 1969 at the age of sixty-seven left his widow almost destitute. "Devil Got My Woman" is Skip James's masterpiece, a chilling wail of lost love from ancestral depths. "Cypress Grove Blues," "Hard Time Killing Floor Blues," and "Special Rider Blues" are other exceptional works. His recordings had a profound effect on Robert Johnson, who adapted two to his own repertoire. Stephen Calt, *Skip James*, *King of the Delta Blues Singers* (Canaan, N.Y.: Biograph Records BLP-12029), notes.

3. Skip James considered himself a serious musician and composer. He advanced his own musical theories and systems in addition to his songwriting and recording. Unlike most bluesmen, James called each of the standard tuning keys by their right names, save for C, which he called "C natural," but which was really E. He also used a rather definite system of string classification. From the sixth string to the first, he termed them: (6) Bass, or Subtone, (5) Baritone, (4) Alto, (3 & 2) Tenors, (1) Soprano. James also refers often to triplets,

16th and 32nd and 64th notes, tonics, subdominants and 2/4 and 4/4 time, all incorrectly. It turns out that he once bought a copy of a book called *Exegesis of Musical Knowledge* from H. C. Speir's shop and looked it over a bit. Al Wilson, "Son House, An Analysis of His Music and a Biography," *Collectors Classics* 14, October 1966.

4. Jack Owens was a friend and musical associate of Skip James who has a small but commanding recording legacy of his own. He has played guitar since childhood and is still considered the best musician around his hometown of Bentonia. He played in the style and tone of this isolated little hilltop town, his songs, like those of James, distinctive for high melismatic singing, complex melodies, intricate guitar parts, and haunting, brooding lyrics dealing with loneliness, death, and the hereafter. Altogether it is one of the eeriest, loneliest, and deepest blues sounds ever recorded. Like James's "Devil Got My Woman," "It Must Have Been the Devil" is Owens's variation on an old Bentonia song theme. David Evans, *It Must Have Been the Devil, Mississippi Country Blues by Jack Owens & Bud Spires* (New York: Testament Records. T-2222), liner notes.

[58]

1. "Choose Your Seat and Set Down" exemplifies the simplicity and solemn dignity of the Afro-American spiritual. It has practical, mundane value as well, serving to usher congregants to their seats as they arrive for their church meetings. An elder of the congregation begins slowly, matching the song precisely to the tenor and tempo of the day. Congregants who already have arrived respond with a faint chorus. The leader sings again, more strongly now. The response is stronger, and soon the spiritual will have gathered all the voices of the church into a swelling, rolling chorus. Each

participant takes his own part from shrillest falsetto to deepest bass and improvises within it. These passionate songs have long comforted the Afro-American with visions of a heavenly reward. The setting and manner of the singing are strongly reminiscent of African religious practice, but the content, flowing out of the Bible and folk hymns of the whites, is distinctly Afro-American. Alan Lomax, *Afro-American Spirituals, Work Songs, and Ballads* (Washington, D.C.: Library of Congress Music Division, AFS L3), descriptive booklet.

2. Refer to note 33:1.

[59]

1. "Our preachers were usually plantation folks, just like the rest of us," most Delta blacks like former slave Robert Anderson would agree, except that the preacher was "called" to his office, called through some religious experience indicating to him that God had chosen him as a spiritual leader, a man who through his personal magnetism or leadership was found worthy of such a position of authority. He was expected to have some knowledge, however imperfect, of the Bible. The fact that he was acquainted with the source of sacred knowledge, which was in a sense the exclusive possession of the whites, gave him prestige in matters concerning religion and the supernatural. He had to be able to communicate his special knowledge to his people, so preaching meant dramatizing the Bible and the way of God to man. The Afro-American preachers of the South—and, later, of urban centers nationwide—were principally known for the imagery of their sermons. The "sermon" moved fluidly from speech to song to dance to moaning and back again. Once more we see the pre-eminence of the *imaginal* over the literal, of images exciting the spirit unto an ecstatic intimacy

with God rather than the mere abstract sense of moral satisfaction, in the Afro-American assimilation of white reality. Rev. J. M. Gates, *I'm Going to Heaven If It Takes My Life* (New York: Riverside Records, SDP 11), discographical notes. Pete Welding, *Singing Preachers and Their Congregations* (Berkeley: America's Music Series No. 19), liner notes.

[60]

1. After an Easter Day service chanted by Sin-Killer Griffin at Darrington State Farm in Sandy Point, Texas, recorded by John A. Lomax in 1934. B. A. Botkin, *Negro Religious Songs and Services* (Washington, D.C.: Library of Congress, Music Division, AFS L10), list of songs.

2. Coupled with the preacher's imaginal sermonizing was his ability to sing; the union of the two skills induced *holy dance* at one or more peaks in a service. The erotic spiritual spasms of this trance state created an image of catharsis, an image of abandonment to God, making holy dance a crucial element of the Delta form of black ecstatic worship. Welding, *Singing Preachers and Their Congregations*.

[64]

1. Robert is singing "I'm Going to Leland," a work song of extraordinary beauty found on Library of Congress LP AAFS L3, recorded by John A. Lomax in 1936 in Parchman, Mississippi. "I went to Leland, Lord, I thought I was lost. . . ."

[67]

1. When Virginia became pregnant in the summer of 1929, Robert became a proud expectant father who now considered himself to be a farmer more than a musician. His

dreams for his wife and family were suddenly destroyed when both Virginia and the baby died in childbirth, in April 1930.

[68]

1. The Yazoo River (Choctaw for "River of Death") starts near Greenwood and runs parallel with U.S. Highway 61 to Redwood, where it diverges and ceases its flow just north of Vicksburg.

[71]

1. In certain isolated spots around the Delta one may still find vestiges of the earliest type of Afro-American religious song, the *ring shout*. True to an ancient West African practice, the dancers shuffle round and round in single file, clapping out the beat in complex counterrhythms. Once an integral part of serious religious observance before its gradual disappearance from the church service or holiness meeting, Delta communities started to reintroduce the ring shout as a means to secure for the Church young people wanting to dance. It soon became permissible for the community to gather in the church on Saturday nights to watch couples promenade around the outside aisle. Alan Lomax, *Afro-American Spirituals, Work Songs, and Ballads*, descriptive booklet.

2. For Calletta Craft, see note 89:1.

[74]

1. According to historian and folklorist Mack McCormick, a striking and very strange characteristic of Robert Johnson was his regular tendency toward sudden changes in

appearance and outlook, oftentimes accompanied by alterations of name and behavior. This made biographical research difficult later on, as few people living today could be sure that it was really Robert Johnson who had crossed their path so long ago.

[76]

1. Neumann, *The Origins and History of Consciousness*, 166.

[78]

1. When Charley Patton documented external events in song, such events were inevitably local ones. "Moon Going Down," one of the fastest pieces in his repertoire, mentions the fiery climax to the Clarksdale cotton mill's demise. By associating this with personal rejection in love, the outward suggestion of incoherence in Patton's songwriting bows to the greater suggestion of alchemical genius, as his images link through rhythm and melody as elements of hallucination. Full of rough human energy, crude and fine and abusive of every rule, this song belongs to the "descending bass" category even though its bass notes have been replaced by thumping or banging sounds. This would be done by hitting the guitar with the right hand and was what Son House referred to as Patton's "clowning." Perls, Calt, et al., *Charley Patton*.

2. George "Bullet" Williams was a recording artist from Selma, Alabama, who was skillful on harmonica. Like many country harmonica players, Williams eschewed melodic concerns for imaginal ones in his recordings, using his harmonica to mock trains ("Frisco Leaving Birmingham") and mimic nature ("The Escaped Convict"). Paul Oliver, *The Story of the Blues* (London: Penguin Books, 1972), 48–49.

3. "Going to Move to Alabama" was Charley Patton's "cover" of one of the biggest hits of the era, Jim Jackson's "Kansas City Blues." The guitar-vocal interplay is brilliant here, the lyrics bizarre ("I got up this mornin' my hat in my hand. / Didn't have no woman or have no man. / I done been to Alabama, graveyard to be her home"). See note 49:2.

[79]

1. Sometime after his twentieth birthday, friends of Robert Johnson remember seeing a "white spot" growing in over part of his left eye. This "spot," which stayed with Robert until the end of his life, was probably a *pterygium* (from the Greek *pteryx*, meaning "wing" or "winglike"), an abnormal mass of mucous membrane growing over the cornea. This affliction is not uncommon among people who spend much of their time outdoors.

2. While they were living for a spell in Cleveland, Mississippi, Bertha Lee had a fight with Charley and cut his throat with a butcher's knife. She would never, of course, discuss the matter, but the story is well known around Cleveland. That Patton survived, with a scar on his throat, and stayed with Bertha Lee is well established. Fahey, *Charley Patton*, 25.

[80]

1. "Stone Pony Blues" was a 1934 remake of Charley Patton's great "Pony Blues" in a different key. Although this number lacked nothing in clarity or precision, the extraordinary relaxed quality of "Pony Blues" seems to degenerate in performance here into laziness or sheer fatigue or an extension of his bodily state. Perls, Calt, et al., *Charley Patton*.

2. This mythical duel between Robert Johnson and Charley Patton, a ritual commonly practiced among Afro-American

musicians as *headhunting* or *headcutting*, is contested with verses from different Charley Patton songs. After Charley opens with three verses from "Stone Pony Blues," Robert challenges him with a stanza from "Pony Blues"; Charley reverts to "Stone Pony" again and is matched by Robert, singing almost the same verse; Charley jumps to "Rattlesnake Blues," Robert picks up the last line Charley sings and rhymes it with a line elsewhere in the song, then Charley struggles through the last verse of "Rattlesnake" to the final word, before conceding defeat.

3. "Walkin' Blues," a seductive boogie with a downbeat that still astonishes, is a popular Robert Johnson song often recorded by blues and rock musicians over the last forty years. A 1942 recording of it by Son House and band at Clack's Store in Lake Cormorant, Mississippi, released on the British Flyright label ("Walking Blues," FLY 541), is a remarkable document of the song as it might have sounded on the street or in the jook.

4. In this scene, young John Shines is spotted by Robert concentrating hard on the performer's musical technique. Competition being what it was, and Robert being ever so self-protective in his enigmatic alienation, he would frequently flee in the middle of a performance if he felt in the least bit paranoid. Both John Shines and David "Honeyboy" Edwards have recalled incidents long ago when they would commence performing with Robert Johnson, only to discover a while later that he had slipped away unnoticed, and often they wouldn't see him again for days or weeks.

[81]

1. In 1933, Charley Patton and Bertha Lee moved to Holly Ridge, where they often performed together locally. Patton was suffering greatly at this time from both his damaged throat and a heart ailment, probably a mitral valve

condition, of which he was soon to die. He was chronically out of breath, and it would take him two or three days to recuperate from a night's singing. Fahey, *Charley Patton*.

[82]

1. Another popular Robert Johnson number, "Sweet Home Chicago" offers a refrain of such peculiar geographical logic as to cause much confused debate among those familiar with the song. The lyrics in question suggest that the singer is asking a girlfriend if she wants to go to "the land of California, my sweet home, Chicago," a place that to most people does not exist. Some people say the reference is to a specific California-to-Illinois train route; the author found this difficult to apply to Delta reality, preferring to think of the refrain as a reference to something of the spirit, of the psyche, a train route of the mind. Recently, however, historian Mack McCormick claimed that Robert had a cousin living in the tiny California town of Port of Chicago. "Sweet Home Chicago" is available on the Columbia LP *Robert Johnson, King of the Delta Blues Singers*, vol. 2, number C 30034.

[83]

1. Friars Point was a town much frequented by itinerant black musicians in the thirties, and Hirsberg's Drugstore there was a favorite gathering place for musicians and audiences. The proprietor of the store, which is still owned and operated by the Hirsberg family, regularly paid musicians to display their wares outside the store in order to attract customers. This was a commonplace practice throughout the South.

2. Friars Point old-timer Lonnie Bass recalls such an incident occurring during a Charley Patton street performance many years ago. Robert was known to draw similarly large and unrestrained crowds as well.

[84]

1. At least one Jackson record shop actually advertised its stock to black laborers this way, and a flyer such as this one did in fact exploit the death of Charley Patton for personal gain. Oliver, *The Story of the Blues*, 106–24.

[85]

1. Charley Patton once made his home in Lula, Mississippi, and wrote a song called "Dry Well Blues" that documented a terrible drought there ("Lord. you oughta been there, Lord. / These womens all leave this town . . .").

2. "The Devil's Dream" is a unique aural vision not unlike nightmare played on ten-note quills, accompanied by snare and bass drums, with vocal effects by Sid Hemphill (see note 38:2). Although there is a well-known British-American fiddle tune called "The Devil's Dream," this performance seems to be but distantly related to its other strain. The fiddle tune here has been transformed into an entirely different instrumental piece. The quills used are panpipes that have been replaced today by the harmonica. Panpipe technique found in "The Devil's Dream" is African in nature, where alternating blown and whooped notes is very common. Images created are dark and discordant, but members of Delta communities are never heard remarking that the music is weird or out of tune. Evans, *Afro-American Folk Music from Tate and Panola Counties, Mississippi*, descriptive brochure.

3. After a sermon delivered by the Rev. F. McGhee in 1930 and found today in America's Music Series *Singing Preachers* collection BC 19, edited by Chris Strachwitz.

4. "If I Had Possession of Judgment Day" is a powerful blues on the traditional "Rollin' and Tumblin'" theme. Robert's

version begins with an unusual religious commentary in the first verse, then follows it with verses also used by Hambone Willie Newbern and Son House. Found on Columbia LP CL 1654.

5. Sin-Killer Griffin's "sermon" here is one that dates back to slavery days and is taken in this instance from a spontaneous sermon rendered by Charley Patton during his recording of "You're Gonna Need Somebody When You Die." The imagery is derived from Revelations.

6. This chant was taken from a field recording made by David and Cheryl Evans titled "Old Dick Jones Is Dead and Gone," performed by Compton Jones and family with "bow diddley" (or "one-string"—see note 16:1), chair, cans, and benches. Issued by the Library of Congress on album AFS L67.

7. Houston Stackhouse reports the story, however apocryphal, that once Robert took an audience away from a singing evangelist by confronting him directly and publicly. If this did, in fact, take place, it would have been a highly unusual occurrence in the timid black Baptist Delta.

[86]

1. Robert Johnson was known to favor a big Gibson guitar in public performance, using another guitar, a Kalamazoo, for special occasions.

[89]

1. Robert Johnson married Calletta Craft at the Copiah County courthouse in May 1931. She was a generous, affectionate woman ten years Robert's senior who had been married twice before and had three small children.

[90]

1. Robert reportedly insisted that his marriage to Calletta be kept a strict secret.

[91]

1. The *ring game* was once a familiar sight among both white and black children in the South. The game was both European and African, with English rhymes and melodies and African rhythms and punctuation. The "Satisfied" theme was a common one. Sometimes the word "satisfied" related meaningfully to the lyrics, other times it related to the rhythm. Ethnic Folkways Library FE 4417, *Negro Folk Music of Alabama*, notes.

[93]

1. John Shines remembered working as a herdsman, tending cows by the riverside. sleeping nights beneath the hood of a car. "The river was full of song," Shines said, "many of it the same as in the fields."

2. "Come On in My Kitchen" is a truly haunting mating call in Spanish tuning, a song in which Robert Johnson's bottleneck guitar follows the vocal line perfectly as it assumes the timbre of the human voice itself. John Shines reported that this song made men and women cry when Robert would play it for them.

[95]

1. All of the great Afro-American musicians of the day came through West Helena, Arkansas, a town just across the Mississippi River from Friars Point. Popular with Mississippians who liked to cross the river for a legal drink, a ferry could be taken for a dime or a skiff for a nickel. Robert Nighthawk,

Roosevelt Sykes, and Hacksaw Harney (see scene 108) were among the many exceptional musicians who gravitated to West Helena.

2. The *Katy Adams* did, in fact, exist, transporting prostitutes who would entice clientele by jiggling coins in the manner described.

[96]

1. Calvin Frazier, who recorded for the Library of Congress in 1938.

[97]

1. William Ferris, *Blues from the Delta* (Garden City, N.Y.: Anchor Press /Doubleday, 1978), photograph.

2. A singer with a recording career almost as prodigious as Lonnie Johnson's, Tampa Red was dubbed "The Guitar Wizard" for his deft playing of the slide guitar (see note 3:4). He was born Hudson Whittaker in Atlanta on Christmas Day, 1900, and spent most of his childhood in Tampa, Florida. In the midtwenties he went to Chicago, where a short stint with Ma Rainey proved to be his breakthrough. It was here that he also met Tom Dorsey, who came to be known as Georgia Tom (see scene 98). Tampa Red stopped the religious Tom from joining the Church by having him set a song he'd written to music. The number turned out to be "It's Tight Like That," and became the first in a series of bawdy commercial hits for the duo. Recognizing a new market in the Southern blacks now living in urban areas who turned away from immediate anxiety for fond remembrances of rural life, Tampa Red formed his Hokum Jug Band, also known as the Hokum Boys. The group was extremely successful and came to be copied by several other "hokum" bands, all of them specializing similarly in good, dirty fun. Tampa Red

continued to perform with new bands such as his Chicago
Five, dazzling all with his rich, ringing guitar and, unlike
Robert Johnson (who had a chordal approach), single-string
melodic runs. He recorded into the 1950s, his work being
available today principally on the RCA-Bluebird and Yazoo
labels. Oliver, *The Story of the Blues*, 100–101.

[98]

1. Frankie "Half-Pint" Jaxon was something of an anomaly in
the world of Afro-American music. Although he was born
in Montgomery, Alabama, in 1895, he was raised in Kansas City, where his shrill feminine voice stood apart from
the local sound. He worked his way through the South
and made a hit in Atlantic City as a female impersonator,
then sang with King Oliver in Chicago at the Sunset Café
and the Plantation. In the late twenties Jaxon hooked up
with Tampa Red, touring and recording with the Hokum
Jug Band. His superior female vocal technique and brilliant sense of timing contributed to making "It's Tight
Like That," "She Loves So Good," and his mockery of Leroy Carr's "How Long How Long Blues" ribald classics. He
later sang with Cow Cow Davenport and the Harlem Ham-
fats, moving from jazz band to vaudeville to hokum Chicago folk blues with considerable ease. Oliver, *The Story of
the Blues*, 67–69.

2. Thomas A. "Georgia Tom" Dorsey was born in Villa Rica,
Georgia, in 1899, and learned to play piano by listening to
the likes of Lark Lee, Soap Stick, and Long Boy perform
in clubs around Atlanta. After failing miserably as a steel-
worker in Gary, Indiana, Dorsey organized a band for Ma
Rainey in Chicago, playing piano for her from that point
on for several years. He met Tampa Red at Ma's last recording session in 1928 and worked with Tampa to introduce a
suave, wry, yet saucy form of urban blues. In 1932, Dorsey's

young wife Nettie died in childbirth while he was on the road. The sorrow-stricken man rushed home to bury her, finding comfort there in his newborn baby girl. Then the baby died also. Dorsey quit blues and jazz altogether, became an ordained Baptist minister, and sang the gospel for over fifty years before his death in 1992. "Precious Lord," a gospel hymn he wrote immediately following his wife's death, is one of the most beautiful spirituals ever composed. Bob Rusch, "Georgia Tom Dorsey—Interview," *Cadence, the American Review of Jazz and Blues*, December 1978. Oliver, *The Story of the Blues*.

[99]

1. According to bluesman Houston Stackhouse, several eminent Delta musicians had formal arrangements with agents for representation.

2. Hacksaw Harney was one of the finest guitarists of his day. See note 95:1.

[103]

1. In 1936, Jackson music shop owner H. C. Speir (see note 10:3), disillusioned by now with the record business and reducing his direct involvement with it, sent word nevertheless to another informal talent scout working in the area, Ernie Oertle, about an impressive young guitar player named Robert Johnson. Oertle was the American Record Company's salesman for the Mid-South in the late 1930s and would audition musicians whose paths crossed with his on his route. After receiving Robert Johnson's name and address from Speir, Oertle sought out the prospect for an audition in the fall of 1936.

2. "Walter 'Buddy Boy' Hawkins was probably born between 1885 and 1900 in Blytheville, Arkansas, where it seems he

spent most of his life; anything else about the man must be inferred from his music, recorded in 1927 and 1929. Because his music is unique and apparently without precedent in the blues idiom, it is precisely in his music that inference becomes difficult. Hawkins used the blues format merely as a framework into which he put contents that might have astonished his contemporaries. His music relied on a harmonic structure far richer than the typical blues piece, with incomparable guitar accompaniments that were *contrapuntally* conceived, usually in four voices. Also, several of his recorded songs betray an unmistakable influence of classical flamenco techniques; one can only speculate where Hawkins came in contact with this music. One guess is that he served in Europe during World War I, as did Son House. Europe had no discernible effect on House's music, but Hawkins may have been more impressionable. Then again, he might have picked it up in New Orleans." According to his introductory jive spoken at the outset of two recordings, Hawkins hailed from Jackson and Birmingham as well as Blytheville. He disappeared without a trace a few years after making his records, and it is doubtful that he is alive today. Jerome Epstein, *Buddy Boy Hawkins and His Buddies* (New York: Yazoo Records, L-1010), liner notes.

[104]

1. "I Believe I'll Dust My Broom" is Robert Johnson's most famous song in the latter-day blues universe, but this is due mainly to the hit record by Elmore James recorded fourteen years later. It is a dance tune that, in Robert's version, powers vigorously to a surging peak in the last two verses. The song was influenced by Leroy Carr's "I Believe I'll Make a Change" and Kokomo Arnold's "Sissy Man Blues," among others. The phrase "dust my broom" here is an idiomatic

expression which means "to leave town." Found on Columbia C 30034.

[105]

1. The rise to power of Emperor Haile Selassie and his Ethiopian empire's invasion by Italy in 1935 created a great deal of interest among Afro-Americans. John Shines told the author that he and Robert discussed Ethiopia on several occasions, with Robert reportedly concerning himself in particular with the place of Ethiopia within a biblical context.

[106]

1. Actually, Oertle drove Robert to San Antonio himself.

2. Don Law represented the American Record Company's Dallas and San Antonio operations back in the 1930s. As head of Columbia Records' Country and Western Division he produced and recorded Bob Wills and Johnny Cash, who called Law his greatest influence as a professional musician.

[109]

1. Robert deserted Calletta, who suffered a severe breakdown and called for her family in Hazlehurst to retrieve her. She died a few years later without ever seeing Robert again.

[110]

1. Southern Afro-American vendors wandering the streets would announce their presence with a rhythmic chant, a semimusical expression that sometimes achieved a haunting, other-worldly, innocent beauty. Two examples of such chanting are to be found on the Riverside LP *A History of*

Classic Jazz (SDP 11), the recordings having been made on the streets of Charleston, South Carolina, in the early part of the twentieth century.

[111]

1. "'Ragtime Texas' Henry Thomas was a singular and important figure in American musical and cultural history. Born in the bottomlands of the Sabine River in East Texas, probably in the mid- to late 1880s, Thomas grew to be a hobo, a vagabond, a big hulking black man whose charismatic singing earned him legendary renown along the Texas & Pacific Railroad line and elsewhere. People still like to remember a time when he came to 'help out' once at a country dance long ago, or they smile to recapture the image of him singing on a sunny street corner somewhere. He walked through hundreds of cities and towns, his clothes and guitar slung onto his back, a soldier in the army of homeless men drifting about the country as they pleased. His musical and cultural heritage was from the final generation of slaves, a major reason why his twenty-three recordings are among the most significant in American musical history. It's good-time music reaching out from another age: reels, anthems, stomps, gospel songs, dance calls, ballads, blues and folk fragments, giving us a blurred glimpse of Afro-American music as it existed in the last century. Thomas' guitar playing was rudimentary, executed with a thrusting drive that evokes a country dance. He used one of the most ancient of all instruments, the panpipe (or 'quills'), to punch out melodies or create natural images. These songs shed a new wisp of half-light on a long lingering mystery: the origin of the blues. He provides varied examples of the idiom at several early stages of development, returning frequently to its most archaic forms. The recordings continually underscore the everlasting irony that so much of America's most expressive

and vital poetry has been composed by an illiterate, uneducated people." Among the finest Ragtime Texas recordings are "Red River Blues," "Honey, Won't You Allow Me One More Chance?," "Woodhouse Blues," "Shanty Blues," "Railroadin' Some," and "Don't Leave Me Here," his final effort. Henry Thomas drifted from view after his 1929 recording sessions, his existence confirmed just one more time—if it really was Thomas on the corner of Crawford and Capitol in Houston during the winter of 1949. The Ragtime Texas legacy has been brilliantly collected and edited, with extensive notes and song annotation, in record and text form. Mack McCormick, *Henry Thomas, "Ragtime Texas"* (Glen Cove, N.Y.: Herwin Records, Herwin 209), biographical notes.

2. "Jonah in the Wilderness" is a narrative gospel song recorded by Henry Thomas in 1927. This is a version of the biblical tale in which Jonah, seen as a reluctant prophet, is not unlike a typical unfaithful or backsliding Christian. One must be familiar with the Book of Jonah to understand this difficult song, while recognizing that, in folk religion, Christian symbols mix fluidly with Old Testament tales. Henry Thomas has chosen to omit the best-known part of the story here, the part in which a "great fish" swallows Jonah and three days later vomits him out onto dry land. Ibid., song annotation.

[112]

1. Directly related in spirit to the black chanting vendors (see note 110:1), black train callers created strangely beautiful aural images with their periodic, unamplified announcements at the train depots. A good example of such a train caller was documented for the Library of Congress in 1936 by John A. Lomax (available on AFS L61).

[116]

1. From *The Blues according to Lightnin' Hopkins*, an essential documentary film by Les Blank.

[117]

1. This recording of "Stormy Weather" is taken from a 1933 Hollywood movie short titled *Bundle of Blues*, made by Paramount Pictures. The vocalist in Duke Ellington's 1933 band here was Miss Ivie Anderson, who was temporarily replaced a year later by Billie Holiday. The LP on which this recording can be found is a limited edition for the Swedish Duke Ellington Society, *Duke Ellington in Hollywood / On the Air, 1933–40*, Max Records (MLP-1001).

[120]

1. "Kindhearted Woman Blues" is an innocently emotive slow blues that, despite its deceptively simple nature, is without compare in the Robert Johnson repertoire. His sudden shift to falsetto voice in the interlude, coupled with several delicate guitar touches of extreme complexity throughout, is remarkable. Found on Columbia LPs CL 1654 and C 30034, in different takes.

[122]

1. According to the daily schedule sheets for the ARC studios in the Gunter Hotel, Adolph and the Bohemians was one of the bands set for rehearsal and recording time along with Robert Johnson's solo "act." The group was one of the many ensembles headed by regional musical stalwart Adolph Hofner, who often worked in tandem with his brother Emil. Hofner became one of the biggest names in western swing and was featured on radio station KTSA in San Antonio.

Richard Stephan Aldrich, *Western Swing*, vol. 2 (Berkeley: Arhoolie Records, Old Timey LP 116), liner notes. Access to the studio schedule sheets provided by Mack McCormick.

2. Robert was to record twenty-nine original songs, and he had numerous others in store and in various stages of development. The record company racial divisions were only interested in an artist's original material, which resulted in a kaleidoscopic array of black popular songs blending in and out of one another through veils of camouflage. Robert's ".32–20 Blues," for example, stands apart from antecedents ".20–20 Blues" by Skip James and Roosevelt Sykes's ".44 Blues," which were recorded years earlier.

3. Robert was born to Julia Dodds and her lover Noah Johnson in Hazlehurst, Mississippi, and spent the first two years of his life in Delta migrant worker camps with his mother. Julia reunited with her husband, Charlie Spencer, in 1914, and with Robert she went to Memphis to live with Spencer as his wife and with her child. When she left Robert and his baby sister Carrie to make it on her own, the young boy faced two more years living with the Spencers before he was able to return to his mother once again in Robinsonville. See notes 1:4 and 4:6.

4. The use of liquor by record companies to heighten the effectiveness of its black recording artists is well known, but its well-regulated place in the proceedings did nothing to hamper their orderly, productive character. In his research, the author found only one instance wherein a singer was "likkered up" so much he could not record, the singer in this case being, not unexpectedly, Tommy Johnson (see note 4:3).

[123]

1. Recording engineers attending to country blues sessions often concerned themselves with the percussive effects of the

feet in a recording. When such sounds were unwanted, pillows were placed underneath the performer's feet as indicated here; if foot-stomping was seen as an aid to the rhythm of a piece, then an extra microphone was deployed near the floor.

[124]

1. "Cross Road Blues" is Robert Johnson's psychodramatic twist to the traditional "traveling blues" theme, a stark and powerful fourteen-bar blues with profoundly evocative imagery. Here we find the innocent singer lost at a backwoods crossroads at sundown, feeling isolated and frightened by the descending darkness. With this work we begin to see Robert's songs emerging as testimony not only to the earthly reality witnessed by the young black songwriter but to his inner psychic landscape as well, by means of the very same words. He performs the song with feverish emotion, biting his images through clenched teeth, growling with spare breath, barely maintaining vocal control. It is the one Robert Johnson song that mentions a real acquaintance of his by name, this person being Robert's "friendboy" Willie Brown (see note 3:2). Many singers have recorded versions of this great song, the most popular rendition having been made by Eric Clapton with his band Cream, a rendition that also includes a verse from Robert's "Traveling' Riverside Blues." Found on Columbia CL 1654 and Roots RL-339.

[125]

1. By 1936 it still could not be assumed that every singer had direct familiarity with a microphone prior to recording, particularly those who lived in such primitive realms as the Afro-American Delta. By listening carefully to Robert Johnson's recordings, one can discern a tendency of his to turn his head away from the microphone in moments of intense

emotion, thereby diminishing the impression of the voice on parts of the recording.

2. Robert Johnson's first issued record featured "Terraplane Blues," a spectacle of guitar and vocal technique and the piece for which he is best remembered in the Delta today. An extraordinary amount of careful preparation went into the creation of this work as is evident by the one-string slide, the rhythmic damping of the strings, the startling shifts to falsetto, and the tight ironic lyrics so well suited for the melody. Upon its release in 1937, "Terraplane Blues" caught the imagination of the Delta community, affecting it rather profoundly. And the unabashed autoeroticism of this driving song's wordplay still makes Buddy McCoy and the boys in Friars Point double over with laughter. Found on Columbia CL 1654.

[126]

1. "Last Fair Deal Gone Down" is a highly rhythmic eight-bar blues bearing distinct elements first found in works by Blind Lemon Jefferson (see note 33:1) and "Ragtime Texas" Henry Thomas (see note 111:1). The primitive, repetitive chanting of the refrain betrays its antiquated roots, as does its subject matter, which places the song's origin in southern Mississippi migrant labor camps. Robert probably first heard the original inspiration for his "Last Fair Deal Gone Down" from his Hazlehurst mentor Ike Zinnerman (see note 22:2). Robert's spontaneous evocation of church bells in the last verse is a lovely surprise. Found on Columbia CL 1654.

[135]

1. At this point in his life, according to both Mack McCormick and John Shines, Robert began to manifest an urgent,

almost obsessive need to meet his natural father, Noah John-son. See note 4:6.

2. After recording the first of what normally would have been two or three takes to "Honeymoon Blues," Robert was in-structed by Don Law to prepare for a second take. Robert's reply, "I want to go with our next one, myself," was etched into the original master recording of the next song and is our only spoken-word document of Robert Johnson. As it turned out, the song that prompted the unusual remark was "Love in Vain."

3. "Love in Vain" is Robert Johnson at his most innocent. The song's character is striking: it is a blues ballad, a love song and lament at once, set to a melody that was floating around the Jackson area in the early 1930s. The origin of the song is ages old, and Ike Zinnerman may have been the one who taught Robert the third verse to "Love in Vain," which also appeared eleven years before in Blind Lemon Jefferson's first record, "Dry Southern Blues." This is Robert Johnson's most celebrated song today, principally because of the worldwide impact of the Rolling Stones' renditions of "Love in Vain" on their *Let It Bleed* and *Get Your Ya-Yas Out!* LPs. Found on Columbia C 30034, with a second take available on Roots RL-339 and Historical HLP-31.

[140]

1. "Me and the Devil Blues" is a slow, sinister, uncannily dra-matic song, a surreal vision of some poor soul waking into the good side of Damnation, a born-again satanic pact con-fessed. The spiritual commitment that pronounced itself first in "Crossroad Blues" and "Stones in My Passway" pro-ceeds in mythic ceremony here. Robert proclaims commu-nion with an "ol' evil spirit," then arrogantly tells one and all where to bury his dead body. See note 164:3. Found on Columbia CL 1654.

[142]

1. This incident actually occurred outside a backwoods café, according to John Shines. Calvin Frazier was wanted by the police for this shooting, so he and his companions fled Mississippi and went northward on the lam for several weeks.

[144]

1. See note 80:4.

[146-147]

1. "Bunk's Place" and "Whitechild's" were two of the many roadside clubs and cafés that Robert might have encountered on the road.

[148]

1. John Shines and Mack McCormick have reported that Robert Johnson formed a combo that might have looked something like this; only the electric pickup on the guitar is questionable. Curiously, Robert was listening to a lot of Bing Crosby's recordings after leaving Texas and was known to perform such numbers as "My Blue Heaven" and "Yes, Sir, That's My Baby" with his band.

[149-150]

1. This incident actually occurred, according to John Shines. Shines noted that it was the only time he ever saw Robert get emotional, let alone cry. And he had never known Robert to play harmonica before, nor did he know that Robert could tap dance. The desperate performance was so successful that the two young men and Calvin Frazier had money enough to buy new guitars.

[151]

1. By 1938, Mississippi's once vigorous lumber industry had fallen into decline, the state's vast woodlands depleted or rendered bare. Federal Writers' Project, *Mississippi*, 109.

[152]

1. A *getback* is a country party or dance, also known as a *frolic*.

2. Three Forks was once a tiny community in the woods between Greenwood and Itta Bena, and today is nothing but an intersection of highways 49E and 82.

3. "Little Queen of Spades" is a celebrated Robert Johnson song of modest melodic inspiration that is filled with lyrical funk. The emotional vocal delivery colors the raunchy images perfectly. The line "Everybody say she got a mojo, 'cause she been usin' that stuff," is a reference to the backwoods brand of Afro-American voodoo (see scene 30 and note 30:1). Found on Columbia C 30034 and Roots RL-339 in different takes.

[157]

1. "Hellhound on My Trail" is unique in Afro-American music not for considerations of structure or melody or style, but for the riveting vividness of its aural imagery. Hailing from a desolate world in which sex is the only salvation, Robert follows here with a song akin to a suicide note, or one that evokes a clear expectation of death. The bodiless voice cries out as if entangled in the discordant guitar strings, the words weave images of sheer despair, the drunken song staggers deliriously downward to a dark spot where trees are trembling, as the frightened voice imagines to the end that a woman will come and save him from all of this. The spiritual instinct of ancient man is vitally evident here in its

grotesque modern guise. The tortured performance is inimitable, with just a couple of "Hellhound" recordings made by others since the original was released. John Shines has told the author, however, that Robert rehearsed the piece so thoroughly that he performed it the same way everywhere he went. There is something awesome about this song. Found on Columbia CL 1654.

[158]

1. Honeyboy Edwards remembers being with Robert Johnson on this fateful night. When he left the party early, too drunk to go on, he was unaware of Robert's poisoning.

[161]

1. Controversy has long enshrouded the death of Robert Johnson. For many years following the murder, scores of rumors in the black community even made the death itself uncertain. As for the cause of death, these rumors generally supposed that a stabbing by some jealous woman was most likely. Over the last decade, however, Mack McCormick has gathered enough evidence—an interview with the murderer included—to conclude reasonably that Robert Johnson was poisoned by a jealous man, as these scenes have imagined.

2. As it was envisaged cinematically, this scene is not complete without the added element of a particular Ethiopian tribal music, a *fila* flute dance. The recording of this trance piece, which is performed by two circles of flute players dancing and chanting in opposite rotations, induces a dark ancestral awareness in the listener that lends the total image a hallucinatory character. Found on the Ocora (Office de Radiodiffusion-Television Française) LP, *Musiques Éthiopiennes*, OCR 75.

[163]

1. Events proceeded in a peculiar manner after Robert's poisoning. He did not die right away, says Mack McCormick, but was taken away in a feeble state by a black man whom no one has ever been able to identify. Our understanding of his name is a phonetic one, and McCormick is not sure if the name is properly pronounced "Tush Hogg" or "Tushogg." In any case, this mysterious fellow took Robert to a little shack and put him to bed, watching over him for three days. When Robert Johnson finally died, he had not yet seen a doctor, so one wonders who this stranger "Tush Hogg" was and why he let Robert die. To make matters worse, McCormick discovered a death certificate signed by Jim Moore, whose identity is also unknown. Maybe Moore drove a white pickup truck.

2. Robert Johnson's family insists that Robert turned his soul over to Jesus Christ just before he died. Robert's half-sister claims to have obtained a slip of linen paper bearing Robert's last words, which confirm this deathbed conversion. The authenticity of the conversion and its written "proof" is doubtful, the meaningfulness of it all negligible, unless placed within the context of myth.

[164]

1. Washington Phillips was born in Freestone County, Texas, around the year 1891. His father Houston Phillips and mother Emma Titas were both native Texans. Between 1927 and 1929, Washington Phillips recorded eighteen songs for a field unit of Columbia Records, which was doing all the gospel recording it would do before the Depression. By recording Blind Willie Johnson at the same time as Phillips, these field units produced the most important Afro-American religious music ever documented on disk (see note 2:2). Phillips's incomparable recordings seem to have been quite successful commercially. Part of his success may

be attributable to his weird sound. He accompanied himself on a *dulceola*, about which an acquaintance of Phillips named Frank Walker has said, "Nobody on earth could use it except him—nobody would want to, I don't think." It was related to the hammered dulcimer, and created a heavenly, childlike sound unlike any instrument anywhere. Beyond this, Phillips was a genuine singer and a fascinating one. About half of his songs on record are traditional, the rest he composed himself, and all of them reflect a common, simple folk morality quite suspicious of the ways of the modern, urbanized world. Phillips ended his short career with "I Had a Good Father and Mother," a song of breathtaking innocence and grace. Very few copies of this record were sold because it was released in the depths of the Depression. With his occupation listed as "farmer," an Austin State Hospital death certificate reveals that Washington Phillips died December 31, 1938, of pulmonary tuberculosis. Since Austin State Hospital was an insane asylum, and since Phillips was treated there for eight years, one month and four days before he died, it is improbable that TB was the main reason for his hospitalization. The fact that the death certificate lists his wife as "unknown" supports this supposition, because families commonly put their mentally deranged away and forgot about them, until recently. Among Washington Phillips's unforgettable recordings are "Take Your Burden to the Lord and Leave It There," "A Mother's Last Word to Her Daughter," "A Mother's Last Word to Her Son," and "Denomination Blues, Parts 1 and 2." Guido van Rijn and Hans Vergeer, *Washington Phillips / "Denomination Blues"* (Ter Aar, Netherlands: Agram Records, Blues AB-2006), liner notes.

2. Toward the end of 1938 John Hammond began lining up performers for his "From Spirituals to Swing" concert. Having heard the ARC recordings of Robert Johnson released on the Vocalion label, Hammond telephoned Don Law in Dallas and asked him to track down the mercurial young

singer and get him to Carnegie Hall somehow. Law was doubtful that Robert could handle the atmosphere and audience, but notified Ernie Oertle nevertheless. It was Oertle who went to Mississippi and sent back the first word of Robert Johnson's death. It might be added that the murder went unreported until 1974, when historian Mack McCormick informed the Greenwood police.

3. Robert Johnson was buried in a pinewood coffin furnished by the county, the grave site located beside the Little Zion Church near Greenwood. Robert's mother and brother-in-law attended his burial.

RECORDINGS USED IN THE RESEARCH AND WRITING OF *LOVE IN VAIN*

Anthologies

Aolt Records 101. *Light Crust Doughboys*. Vol. 1. Produced by Ray Doggett.

Arhoolie Records: Old Timey LP 116. *Western Swing*. Vol. 2 (Jimmie Revard, Milton Brown, Light Crust Doughboys, Adolph Hofner, W. Lee O'Daniel, Washboard Wonders, Bob Wills). Edited by Chris Strachwitz.

BC LP No. 19. *Negro Religious Music*. Vol. 3, *Singing Preachers and Their Congregations* (Rev. D. C. Rice, Rev. F. McGhee, Elder Otis Jones, Elder Lightfoot Solomon Michaux, Rev. Kelsey, Rev. C. C. Chapman). Edited by Chris Strachwitz.

Biograph BLP-12027. *This Old World's in a Hell of a Fix* (The Gospel according to Skip James, Fred McDowell, Robert Wilkins, Black Billy Sunday, Jaybird Coleman, Washington Phillips).

Ethnic Folkways Library FE 4417. *Negro Folk Music of Alabama—Secular*. Recorded in Alabama by Harold Courlander.

Folklyric Records 9004. *Corridos, Part 1: 1930–1934* (Hermanos Bañuelos, Pedro Rocha and Lupe Martinez, Nacho and Justino, Hermanos Sanchez and Linares). Edited by Chris Strachwitz.

Folkways Records FJ-2807. *Jazz New York: 1922–34* (Louis Armstrong, Jack Teagarden, Duke Ellington, Fletcher Henderson, Fats Waller, Louisiana Rhythm Kings).

Folkways Records FS 3841. *See Island Folk Festival* (Moving Star Hall Singers and Alan Lomax).

Historical Records, Melodeon MLP 7324. *Party Blues* (Tampa Red's Hokum Jug Band, Red Nelson, Bo Carter, Blind Blake, John Hurt, Memphis Jug Band).

Library of Congress, Music Division, Recording Laboratory, AFS L3. *Folk Music of the United States: Afro-American Spirituals, Work Songs, and Ballads* (from the Archive of American Folk Song). Edited by Alan Lomax.

Library of Congress, Music Division, Recording Laboratory, AFS L10. *Folk Music of the United States: Negro Religious Songs and Services* (from the Archive of American Folk Song). Edited by B. A. Botkin.

Library of Congress, Music Division, Recording Laboratory, AFS L4. *Folk Music of the United States: Afro-American Blues and Game Songs* (from the Archive of American Folk Song). Edited by Alan Lomax.

Library of Congress, Music Division, Recording Laboratory, AFS L67. *Afro-American Folk Music from Tate and Panola Counties, Mississippi* (from the Archive of American Folk Song). Edited by David Evans.

New World Records NW-252. *Roots of the Blues* (Lining Hymn and Prayer, Church-House Moan, Field Song from Senegal).

Ocora Records OCR 75. *Musiques Éthiopiennes* (Office de Radiodiffusion-Television Française). Directed by Charles Duvelle.

Ocora Records 558511. *Burundi: Musiques Traditionnelles*, with the cooperation of the Voice of the Revolution of Burundi, OCR 40.

Origin OJL-5. *The Mississippi Blues 1927–1940* (John Hurt, Bukka White, Willie Brown, Son House, William Harris).

Origin OJL-13. *In the Spirit*. Vol. 2 (Mother McCollum, Blind Willie Johnson, Washington Phillips, Charley Patton).

RBF Records RBF-14. *Blues Roots: Mississippi* (Tommy Johnson, Bo Carter, Joe Williams, Robert Johnson, Tommy McClennan, Robert Petway, Mississippi Jook Band).

Riverside Records SDP-II. *History of Classic Jazz* (Rev. J. M. Gates, Blind Lemon Jefferson, Street Cries of Charleston–1926, Ida Cox, Chippie Hill, Georgia Camp Meeting, Cripple Clarence Lofton).

Roots RL-314. *Mississippi Blues*. Vol. 3 (Poor Boy Lofton's "Jake Leg Blues," Robert Johnson, John Hurt, Robert Petway, Bo Carter, Mississippi Sheiks, Tommy McClennan). Limited Edition. Roots RL-339. *Delta Blues* (Robert Johnson, Skip James, Son House, Charley Patton). Limited edition.

Roots Special Edition RSE-5. *Legendary Sessions, Delta Style* (Willie Brown, Son House, Louise Johnson). Collectors' Series.

Rounder Records 2014. *Get Your Ass in the Water and Swim Like Me! (Narrative Poetry from Black Oral Tradition)*. Recorded and edited by Bruce Jackson.

Stash ST-101. *Copulatin' Blues—Vol.* 2 (Sidney Bechet, Lil Johnson, Bessie Smith, Coot Grant, Tampa Red's Hokum Band, Jelly Roll Morton, Lucille Bogan).

Yazoo Records L-1004. *Tex-Arkana-Louisiana Country 1929–1933* (Buddy Boy Hawkins, Henry Thomas, Texas Alexander, King Solomon Hill). Edited by Stephen Calt.

Individual Artists

Ellington, Duke. *In Hollywood / On the Air 1933–40*. Members of the Duke Ellington Society, Max Records MLP-1001. Limited edition.

House, Son. *The Legendary 1941–1942 Recordings in Chronological Sequence* (including Willie Brown, Fiddlin' Joe Martin). Folklyric 9002.

James, Skip. *King of the Delta Blues Singers*. Biograph BLP-12029.

Johnson, Blind Willie. *Blind Willie Johnson 1927–1930*. RBF Records RBF-10.

———. *Blind Willie Johnson, His Story Told, Annotated and Documented by Samuel B. Charters*. Folkways Records FG-3585.

Johnson, Lonnie. *Mr. Johnson's Blues 1926–1932*. Mamlish Records S-3807.

Johnson, Robert. *King of the Delta Blues Singers*. Vol. 1. Thesaurus of Classic Jazz. Columbia CL 1654.

———. *King of the Delta Blues Singers*. Vol. 2. Columbia C 30034.

Johnson, Tommy. *The Famous 1928 Tommy Johnson–Ishman Bracey Session*. Roots RL-330.

Owens, Jack. *Mississippi Country Blues*. With Bud Spires. Testament Records T-2222.

Patton, Charley. *Charley Patton, Founder of the Delta Blues*. Yazoo L-1020.

———. *Patton, Sims, and Bertha Lee—Bottleneck Guitar Pioneer*. Herwin Records 213.

Phillips, Washington. *Denomination Blues*. Agram Records, Blues AB-2006.

Thomas, Henry. *Ragtime Texas—Complete Recorded Works, 1927–1929*. Herwin Records 209. Notes by Mack McCormick.

Wilkins, Rev. Robert. *Memphis Gospel Singer*. Including "Prodigal Son." Music Research Inc., Piedmont Records PLP-13162.

PERMISSIONS

"Come On in My Kitchen"
Words and music by Robert Johnson
Copyright © (1978), 1990, 1991 MPCA King of Spades (SESAC)
and Claud L. Johnson (SESAC)
Administered by MPCA Music LLC

"Cross Road Blues (Crossroads)"
Words and music by Robert Johnson
Copyright © (1978), 1990, 1991 MPCA King of Spades (SESAC)
and Claud L. Johnson (SESAC)
Administered by MPCA Music LLC

"From Four Until Late"
Words and music by Robert Johnson
Copyright © (1978), 1990, 1991 MPCA King of Spades (SESAC)
and Claud L. Johnson (SESAC)
Administered by MPCA Music LLC

"Hell Hound on My Trail"

Words and music by Robert Johnson

Copyright © (1978), 1990, 1991 MPCA King of Spades (SESAC)
and Claud L. Johnson (SESAC)

Administered by MPCA Music LLC

Reprinted by permission of Hal Leonard Corporation

"I Believe I'll Dust My Broom"

Words and music by Robert Johnson

Copyright © (1978), 1990, 1991 MPCA King of Spades (SESAC)
and Claud L. Johnson (SESAC)

Administered by MPCA Music LLC

Reprinted by permission of Hal Leonard Corporation

"If I Had Possession over Judgment Day"

Words and music by Robert Johnson

Copyright © (1978), 1990, 1991 MPCA King of Spades (SESAC)
and Claud L. Johnson (SESAC)

Administered by MPCA Music LLC

Reprinted by permission of Hal Leonard Corporation

"Last Fair Deal Gone Down"

Words and music by Robert Johnson

Copyright © (1978), 1990, 1991 MPCA King of Spades (SESAC)
and Claud L. Johnson (SESAC)

Administered by MCPA Music LLC

Reprinted by permission of Hal Leonard Corporation

"Little Queen of Spades"

Words and music by Robert Johnson

Copyright © (1978), 1990, 1991 MPCA King of Spades (SESAC)
and Claud L. Johnson (SESAC)

Administered by MPCA Music LLC

Reprinted by permission of Hal Leonard Corporation

"Love in Vain Blues"

Words and Music by Robert Johnson

Copyright © (1978), 1990, 1991 MPCA King of Spades (SESAC)
and Claud L. Johnson (SESAC)

Administered by MPCA Music LLC

Reprinted by permission of Hal Leonard Corporation

"Me and the Devil Blues"

Words and music by Robert Johnson

Copyright © (1978), 1990, 1991 MPCA King of Spades (SESAC)
and Claud L. Johnson (SESAC)

Administered by MPCA Music LLC

Reprinted by permission of Hal Leonard Corporation

"Preachin' Blues (Up Jumped the Devil)"

Words and music by Robert Johnson

Copyright © (1978), 1990, 1991 MPCA King of Spades (SESAC)
and Claud L. Johnson (SESAC)

Administered by MPCA Music LLC

Reprinted by permission of Hal Leonard Corporation

"Terraplane Blues"
Words and music by Robert Johnson
Copyright © (1978), 1990, 1991 MPCA King of Spades (SESAC)
and Claud L. Johnson (SESAC)
Administered by MPCA Music LLC

ALAN GREENBERG is a writer, film director, film producer, and photographer. He worked on Martin Scorsese's *Cape Fear* and Bernardo Bertolucci's *1900* and with Werner Herzog on his classic screenplays *Fitzcarraldo, Cobra Verde,* and *Heart of Glass.* His documentary *Land of Look Behind* received the Chicago International Film Festival's Gold Hugo award. He is the author of *Every Night the Trees Disappear: Werner Herzog and the Making of "Heart of Glass."*

MARTIN SCORSESE is an Academy Award–winning director, screenwriter, producer, actor, and film historian. A recipient of the AFI Life Achievement Award, he is considered one of America's most influential filmmakers. He was executive producer for the acclaimed seven-part film series *The Blues.*

STANLEY CROUCH is a columnist, novelist, and essayist. His writing has been published in *Harper's,* the *New York Times, Vogue, Downbeat,* and the *New Yorker.* He is a founder of Jazz at Lincoln Center, where he has been artistic consultant for jazz programming since 1987. He is author of *Considering Genius: Jazz Writings.*